FOLLOW ME

BIBLE STUDY

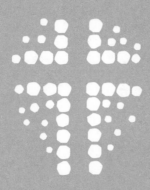

DAVID PLATT

LifeWay Press®
Nashville, Tennessee

Published by LifeWay Press®
© 2013 David Platt
Reprinted 2013

ISBN 978-1-4158-7645-9
Item 005541907

Dewey decimal classification: 248.84
Subject headings: DISCIPLESHIP \ CHRISTIAN LIFE \
JESUS CHRIST

Photo of David Platt: Allison Lewis

To order additional copies of this resource, write to LifeWay
Church Resources Customer Service; One LifeWay Plaza;
Nashville, TN 37234-0113; order online at *www.lifeway.com*;
fax 615.251.5933; email *orderentry@lifeway.com*; phone toll free
800.458.2772; or visit the LifeWay Christian Store serving you.

Printed in the United States of America

Adult Ministry Publishing
LifeWay Church Resources
One LifeWay Plaza
Nashville, TN 37234-0152

CONTENTS

THE AUTHOR

Dr. David Platt, the pastor of The Church at Brook Hills, is deeply devoted to Christ and His Word. David's first love in ministry is disciple making—the simple, biblical model of teaching God's Word, mentoring others, and sharing faith. He's traveled extensively to teach the Bible alongside church leaders throughout the United States and around the world.

David has authored several books, including *Radical, Radical Together,* and *Follow Me*. He's the founder of Radical *(Radical.net),* a resource ministry dedicated to serving the church in making disciples of all nations.

David and his wife, Heather, have four children: Caleb, Joshua, Mara Ruth, and Isaiah.

INTRODUCTION

"Follow me." Jesus spoke those words two thousand years ago to a group of fishermen, and they answered. They followed, and they changed the world. Today Jesus is still speaking those words to us. Will we answer? Will we follow?

This call to follow Christ is inevitably a call to die. That's been clear since the beginning of Christianity. In the footsteps of Jesus, the first disciples found a path worth giving their lives to tread. Two thousand years later, I wonder how far we've wandered from that path.

Somewhere along the way, amid varying cultural tides and popular church trends, it seems we've minimized Jesus' summons to total abandonment. Churches are filled with people who seem content to have a casual association with Jesus and to give nominal adherence to His commands. Scores of men, women, and children have been told that becoming a follower of Jesus simply involves believing certain truths or saying certain words.

This isn't true. The call to follow Jesus isn't simply an invitation to pray a prayer; it's a summons to lose your life.

That's why I've written this study. In a previous book, *Radical,* I sought to expose ideas that are common in our culture (and in the church) yet antithetical to the gospel. My aim was to identify thoughts and values of this world that we must let go of to follow Jesus.

The purpose of this study is to take the next step. I want to move from *what* we let go of to *Whom* we hold on to. I want to explore not only the gravity of what we must forsake in this world but also the greatness of the One we follow in this world—for there is indescribable joy to be found, deep satisfaction to be felt, and an eternal purpose to be fulfilled in dying to ourselves and living in Him. Are you ready to answer the call?

HOW TO GET THE MOST FROM THIS STUDY

1. **ATTEND EACH GROUP EXPERIENCE.**
    - **Watch the DVD teaching.**
    - **Participate in the group discussions.**
2. **COMPLETE THE MATERIAL IN THIS WORKBOOK.**
    - **Read the daily lessons and complete the learning activities.**
    - **Memorize each week's suggested memory verse.**
    - **Be honest with yourself and others about your thoughts, your questions, and your experiences as you study and apply the material.**
    - **Ask God to show you His truth about each topic so that you can be confident you're following Jesus as the Lord of your life.**
3. **OBTAIN AND READ THE BOOK *FOLLOW ME* by David Platt.**
    - **Tyndale, 2013, ISBN 978-1-4143-8241-8**

THE CALL

Welcome to this group discussion of *Follow Me*.

4/28/14

To facilitate introductions and to introduce the theme of *Follow Me,* work as a group to form a one-sentence definition of what it means to follow Christ—what it means to live as a Christian in today's society. Use the questions below to guide your discussion while forming this definition.

What ideas or images come to mind when you hear the word *Christian*? Why?

good PRINCIPLES, BELIEVER, FOLLOWER

Describe what most Christians today see as their purpose in life.

LEAD OTHERS TO CHRIST

What are the primary goals Christians should strive to achieve while living and working in the world?

Record your group's final definition.

A Christian is:

*Love God HEART, MIND, SOLE
TRANSFORMING SOMEBODY ELSE*

To prepare to view the DVD segment, read aloud Matthew 4:17-20:

> **From that time on Jesus began to preach, "Repent, for the kingdom of heaven is near." As Jesus was walking beside the Sea of Galilee, he saw two brothers, Simon called Peter and his brother Andrew. They were casting a net into the lake, for they were fishermen. "Come, follow me," Jesus said, "and I will make you fishers of men." At once they left their nets and followed him.**

WATCH

Complete the viewer guide below as you watch DVD session 1.

From the very beginning, Matthew makes it clear that Jesus is the _SAVIOR_,
the Messiah.

Jesus is the Sovereign over the wise and the _SHEPHERD_ of the weak.

Jesus is the Savior King and the Righteous _JUDGE_.

Jesus is the new Adam and the true _ISRAEL_.

Jesus is clearly, absolutely worthy of far more than church attendance and casual
ASSOCIATION.

Jesus is worthy of total abandonment and supreme _ADORATION_.

To follow Jesus means to live with radical _ABANDONMENT_ for His glory.

To _REPENT_ means to confess your sin, to express sorrow over your sin, to turn
from your sin, and ultimately to renounce yourself.

Followers of Jesus don't always know all the details about where they're going, but they
always know _WHO_ they're with.

When you become a follower of Jesus, you lose your _LIFE_ as you know it.

To follow Jesus is to lay down all of these things in order to live for one thing: to honor
the _KING_.

To follow Jesus is to live with radical abandonment for His glory and to live with joyful
DEPENDENCE on His grace.

To follow Jesus is to live with faithful _ADHERENCE_ to His person.

To follow Jesus is to live with total _TRUST_ in His sovereign, supreme authority
in every domain and over every detail in your life.

To follow Jesus is to live with urgent _OBEDIENCE_ to His mission.

Video sessions available for purchase at *www.lifeway.com/followme*

Discuss the DVD segment with your group, using the questions below.

What did you like best from David's teaching? Why?

Review your earlier definition of what it means to follow Christ in today's culture. What would you change after hearing David's teaching?

How is Jesus viewed and portrayed in Western culture? *[handwritten: good teacher, our savior to get into heaven]*

How is Jesus viewed and portrayed in the church? *[handwritten: Lord Savior of the one ways to god]*

Respond to David's statement: "You and I have nothing in us to draw Jesus to us, to give us this invitation. We are sinners, rebels to the core running from God. And the beautiful, gracious, glorious reality of the gospel is that Jesus comes running to us."

What emotions do you experience when you hear the word *evangelism*? Why? *[handwritten: being lead to Jesus, driving it home!]*

Are you currently making disciples of Jesus? Explain.

Application: Before concluding this group discussion, make a list of five people from your sphere of influence who aren't following Christ. Commit to praying daily for each of these people throughout this week, asking the Holy Spirit to convict them of their sin and their need to experience salvation.

Scripture: Memorize Matthew 4:19-20 this week.

_____

[handwritten:
Gary C.
Carolyn W.
Greg
Liz]

READ week 1 and complete the activities before the next group experience.
READ chapters 1–2 in the book *Follow Me* by David Platt (Tyndale, 2013).

This Week's Scripture Memory

**"Come, follow me," Jesus said, "and I will make you fishers of men."
At once they left their nets and followed him. Matthew 4:19-20**

When we look back at the flow of history, we can identify a number of unique and critical turning points—events that not only impacted the world as they happened but also fundamentally changed everything that happened afterward. Today we refer to these events as watershed moments.

For example, the invention of the printing press in 1436 was unquestionably a watershed moment. Through the mass production of books, Johannes Gutenberg was instrumental in both the Protestant Reformation and the Scientific Revolution. Similarly, the assassination of Archduke Ferdinand in 1914 sparked World War I, which in turn created the political conditions leading to World War II.

The Bible records another watershed moment in Matthew 4: Jesus' calling of His first disciples. It was a simple event, relatively speaking. Walking along the Sea of Galilee in ancient Israel, Jesus encountered two sets of brothers working as fishermen. He asked them to drop what they were doing and follow Him as disciples instead. They answered His call. They followed.

This decision was certainly a watershed moment for those four men. Doing so changed everything about their lives from that day forward. But it was also a watershed moment in a much broader sense, because the impact of that decision still reverberates throughout human history. Through the power of God, they became part of a movement that's literally reshaped the course of human history and impacted billions of people throughout the following centuries, including you and me.

This week we'll focus on that moment when Jesus first called His disciples, along with several more of their experiences and encounters during His public ministry. Ultimately, we'll find answers to this important question: What does it mean to truly follow Jesus?

THE CALL

THE COST

Imagine a woman named Ayan. She's part of a community that prides itself on being 100 percent Muslim. To belong to Ayan's tribe is to be a Muslim. Ayan's personal identity, familial honor, relational standing, and social status are all inextricably intertwined with Islam. Simply put, if Ayan ever leaves her faith, she'll immediately lose her life. If Ayan's family ever found out that she was no longer a Muslim, they'd kill her without question or hesitation.

Now imagine having a conversation with Ayan about Jesus. You start by telling her God loves her so much that He sent His only Son to die on the cross for her sins as her Savior. As you speak, you sense her heart softening toward what you're saying. At the same time, you feel her spirit trembling as she contemplates what it would cost for her to follow Christ.

With fear in her eyes and faith in her heart, she looks at you and asks, "How do I become a Christian?"

How would you answer that question?

Has your answer to that question changed over the course of your life? Why or why not?

There are really only two ways to answer Ayan's question. The first way is to tell her how easy it is to become a Christian. If Ayan will simply assent to certain truths and repeat a particular prayer, she can be saved. That's all it takes.

Your second option is to tell Ayan the truth. You can tell her through the gospel, God has called her to die. Literally. To die to her life. To die to her family. To die to her friends. To die to her future.

But there's more. In dying, God has called her to live in Jesus as part of a global family that includes every tribe, tongue, and nation. He's called her to live with friends who span every age. He's called her to find a future in which joy will last forever.

Ayan isn't imaginary. She's a real woman who made a real choice to become a Christian—to die to herself and live in Christ, no matter the cost. Because of her decision, she was forced to flee her family and friends. Yet she's now working strategically and sacrificially to spread the gospel among her people.

The Cost Is High

What does it mean to truly, biblically follow Christ? And what does it mean to follow Him, not only in a hostile community like Ayan's but also in a place of relative comfort and security like America? What does it mean to know Jesus and identify your life with His? In short, what does it mean to be a Christian?

These are vitally important questions, and these are some of the subjects we'll explore throughout this study. To get started, let's take a look at how Jesus called His first disciples:

> **As Jesus was walking beside the Sea of Galilee, he saw two brothers, Simon called Peter and his brother Andrew. They were casting a net into the lake, for they were fishermen. "Come, follow me," Jesus said, "and I will make you fishers of men." At once they left their nets and followed him. Going on from there, he saw two other brothers, James son of Zebedee and his brother John. They were in a boat with their father Zebedee, preparing their nets. Jesus called them, and immediately they left the boat and their father and followed him. Matthew 4:18-22**

What strikes you as most interesting in these verses? Why?

I think it's fair to say Peter, Andrew, James, and John didn't have a complete understanding of what they were getting themselves into. They didn't fully grasp that Jesus was beckoning them to leave behind their professions, possessions, dreams, ambitions, family, friends, safety, and security—to abandon everything to follow Him.

But Jesus made sure to fill them in later:

> **Jesus said to his disciples, "If anyone would come after me, he must deny himself and take up his cross and follow me. For whoever wants to save his life will lose it, but whoever loses his life for me will find it." Matthew 16:24-25**

What does it mean for a person to deny himself or herself?

How would the people of Jesus' day have understood the phrase "take up his cross" (v. 24)?

How do we understand that phrase in today's culture?

In a world where everything revolves around self—protect yourself, promote yourself, preserve yourself, take care of yourself—Jesus said, "Slay yourself." And that's exactly what happened. According to Scripture and tradition, those four fishermen paid a steep price for following Jesus. Peter was hung upside down on a cross, Andrew was crucified in Greece, James was beheaded, and John was exiled.

Make no mistake about it: the cost of following Jesus is high. Whether we live in northern Africa or Beverly Hills, to become a Christian means to lose our lives.

How have you experienced the high cost of following Jesus?

The Reward Is Worth It

Peter, Andrew, James, and John believed following Jesus was worth the cost—even worth the loss of their freedom and their lives. Why? Because they received Jesus. They exchanged *their* lives for *His* life, and the results of that exchange were totally in their favor. In Jesus these men discovered a love that surpassed comprehension, a satisfaction that superseded circumstances, and a purpose that transcended every other possible pursuit in this world. They eagerly, willingly, and gladly lost their lives in order to know, follow, and proclaim Christ.

Can the same be said of you and me? That's another question we need to answer in this study.

What benefits have you received from your relationship with Christ? Record three of the most valuable to you.

1.

2.

3.

I invite you to join me on a journey in the pages ahead. I don't claim to have all of the answers, nor do I understand everything that following Jesus entails. But in a day when the basics of becoming and being a Christian are maligned by the culture and misunderstood in the church, the Bible makes it clear there's more to following Jesus than the routine religion we're tempted to settle for.

What do you hope to learn or experience about following Jesus as you participate in this study?

I'm convinced that when we take a serious look at what Jesus really meant when He said "Follow Me," we'll discover there's far more pleasure to be experienced in Him than in anything else. There's indescribably greater power to be realized with Christ and a much higher purpose to be accomplished for Him than in anything else this world has to offer.

As a result, all of us—every Christian—can be set free to eagerly, willingly, and gladly lose our lives in order to know and proclaim Christ.

THAT'S WHAT IT MEANS TO FOLLOW HIM.

DON'T INVITE JESUS INTO YOUR HEART

I'll never forget the day I received an e-mail from our adoption agency with a picture of a little boy. Nine months old. Abandoned at birth. In need of a home, a mom, and a dad. I printed the picture and ran to show it to Heather. We laughed, we cried, we rejoiced, we prayed, and within two weeks we were on a plane headed to Kazakhstan.

We arrived the day after Valentine's Day in 2006 and were immediately taken to the orphanage. The director was sharing all kinds of medical information with us when it happened: a woman rounded the corner with a precious 10-month-old boy in her arms. Words can't describe the swell of emotion in that room as the woman handed him to us, and for the first time Caleb Platt looked into the eyes of a mom and a dad.

We stayed in Kazakhstan for four weeks, holding our son, feeding him, singing to him, laughing with him, and crawling on the floor with him. Finally, we stood in front of a judge and heard those wonderful words: "I grant this application of adoption, and this child now belongs to David and Heather Platt."

What words or images come to mind when you hear the word *adoption?*

The Right Pursuit

The parallels between Caleb's story and the gospel story are many, but I want to point out one that's particularly significant: adoption like this begins with a parent's initiative, not a child's idea. Our 10-month-old boy didn't invite us to come to Kazakhstan and bring him into our family, for he didn't even know to ask for such a thing. No, this orphaned child became our cherished son because of a love that was entirely beyond his imagination and completely outside his control.

Caleb didn't pursue us, for he was utterly unable to do so. Instead, we pursued him.

This is the heart of Christianity, and we're prone to miss it if we describe becoming a Christian as "inviting Jesus into your heart." We don't become followers of Christ by pursuing Christ or inviting Christ to do anything, for in our sin we're totally unable to do so. Instead, we become Christians when Christ pursues us and invites us to follow Him.

What's your reaction to the previous paragraph? Why?

Jesus made this clear when He spoke to His disciples at the last supper:

You did not choose me, but I chose you and appointed you to go and bear fruit—fruit that will last. Then the Father will give you whatever you ask in my name. This is my command: Love each other. John 15:16-17

What emotions do you experience when you read these verses? Why?

What does it mean that God "chose you and appointed you to go and bear fruit"?

Sometimes I ask people, "How do you know you're a Christian?" or "How do you know you're saved from your sin?" The most common replies I hear from professing Christians are "Because I decided to trust in Jesus," "Because I prayed and asked Jesus to come into my heart many years ago," or even "Because I've given my life to Jesus."

Notice how each reply begins with the words, "Because I ..." Such responses aren't wrong, and I assure you my aim is not to be the word police, but I do want to offer what I hope is a healthy reminder that you and I are not saved from our sin primarily because *we* decided to do something a certain number of years ago. Instead, we're saved from our sin ultimately because *Jesus* decided to do something two thousand years ago. And based on His grace, His mercy, and His love in coming to us—sinners totally unable to save ourselves—we've been invited to follow Him.

In other words, the love of God in the life and death of Jesus Christ is the only foundation for authentic salvation.

In the past have you thought of your salvation in terms of something you did or something Jesus did? Why?

God's Shocking Grace

Maybe you're wondering whether these distinctions really matter: *Is it really important to specify that Christ chose us instead of the other way around? Does it really make a difference if we adjust our understanding in this way?*

The answer to those questions is yes. It matters that we understand what Christ has done for us. It's important. And the reason it's important is because of our sin.

What ideas or images come to your mind when you hear the word *sin*?

For too long we in the church have convinced one another that we're basically good people who occasionally make some bad decisions. Whether we've lied, cheated, stolen, or taken God's name in vain, we simply tell ourselves we've all made mistakes. And the solution is easy: just invite Jesus to come into your heart, and He will forgive you of all these things before you can say, "Amen."

This thinking is false. At our very core we're enemies of God with no real desire to know Him. We're utterly unable to call on Christ because we're totally consumed with running from the Father. That's what it means to be sinful. And if you think I'm overstating this a little bit, look at the testimony of God's Word:

• In our sin we've alienated ourselves from God and are hostile toward Him (see Col. 1:21).

• We're slaves to our sin (see John 8:34) and dominated by Satan (see 2 Tim. 2:26).

• We love darkness and hate light (see John 3:20; Eph. 4:18).

• We live in impurity and lawlessness (see Rom. 6:19).

• Our minds are depraved (see Rom. 1:28) and blinded to truth by the god of this world (see 2 Cor. 4:4).

• Our emotions are disordered, our hearts are sinful (see Rom. 1:26), and the wicked passions of our flesh wage war against our souls (see 1 Pet. 2:11).

• Our bodies are defiled (see Rom. 1:24); we are morally evil (see Gen. 8:21) and spiritually sick (see Matt. 9:12).

How have you seen these realities expressed in your life?

Read the following passages of Scripture and record what they teach about our sinful condition.

Isaiah 64:6-7

Romans 3:9-18

Ephesians 2:1-3

Understand this: as members of the human race, we're filthy in our sinfulness. We're utterly repulsive to our perfect Creator. And yet our perfect Creator chose to save us anyway. Moreover, He *wants* us! He wants us to be His children!

Before being saved, all of us were dead in our transgressions. We had no signs of life and no hope of any blessing for eternity. And yet God moved heaven and earth to offer us eternal life. He gave His own life to rescue us, give us life, and make us His own. That's the message of the gospel.

Do you see why the idea of casually inviting Jesus to join our lives is contrary to the message of the gospel? And do you see why we must have a proper understanding of our situation to properly appreciate and worship our King?

What are more appropriate ways to describe salvation?

Does your life reflect an appreciation for the shocking grace you've received? Why or why not?

Perhaps now you're wondering whether we as human beings have any part at all in the process of salvation: *Surely the searching love of God must be believed and received. God isn't the only one working in salvation. We must choose to accept or reject God's mercy in Christ, right?*

Absolutely. The mystery of God's mercy in no way negates a person's responsibility in salvation. This entire Bible study revolves around the decision each one of us makes to follow Jesus.

Ultimately, however, to be a Christian is to be loved by God, pursued by God, and found by God. To be a Christian is to realize that in your sin you were separated from God's presence and deserved nothing but God's wrath.

YET DESPITE YOUR DARKNESS AND IN YOUR DEADNESS,

HIS LIGHT SHONE ON YOU, AND HIS VOICE

SPOKE TO YOU, INVITING YOU TO **FOLLOW** HIM.

UNDERSTANDING SALVATION

I have a friend—let's call him John—whose first exposure to the concept of hell was during an episode of "Tom and Jerry" when he was young. During one particularly vivid scene, Tom was sent to hell for something bad he'd done to Jerry. What was intended to be a humorous cartoon ended up scaring John to death, and he later found himself at church talking with a man about what he'd seen.

The churchgoer looked at John and said, "Well, you don't want to go to hell, do you?"

"No," John responded.

"OK then," the man said. "Pray this prayer after me. Dear Jesus …"

John paused. After some awkward silence he realized he was supposed to repeat after the man. So he hesitantly responded, "Dear Jesus …"

"I know I'm a sinner, and I know Jesus died on a cross for my sins," the man said. John repeated his words.

"I ask You to come into my heart and save me from my sin," the man said. Again, John echoed what he'd heard.

"Amen," the man concluded. Then the man looked at John and said, "Son, you're saved from your sins, and you don't ever have to worry about hell again."

What emotions did you experience when you read the previous conversation? Why?

Away from Me

Surely what that man told my friend in church that day wasn't true. Surely this isn't what it means to respond to Jesus' invitation to follow Him—and yet these kinds of conversations are repeated year after year within the church.

Shouldn't it alarm us that such simplistic pathways to Christianity are nowhere to be found in God's Word? Shouldn't we who follow Christ be concerned that the Scriptures contain no references to people asking Jesus into their hearts or reciting a prayer of salvation?

Yet this is exactly what multitudes of professing Christians have been encouraged to do. Worse, they've been assured that as long as they asked Jesus into their heart, invited Him into their life, prayed a prayer, raised their hand, signed a card, or walked an aisle, they're Christians, and their salvation is eternally secure.

It's a lie. With good intentions and a sincere desire to reach as many people as possible for Christ, we've subtly and deceptively minimized the magnitude of what it means to follow Jesus. As a result, multitudes of men and women at this moment think they're saved from their sins when they aren't. Scores of people around the world culturally identify themselves as Christians when biblically they aren't.

What's your reaction to the previous statements? Why?

What evidence have you encountered to support the idea that many people who claim to be Christians aren't actually following Jesus?

I realize these claims may be surprising for a lot of people, perhaps even offensive. You may be wondering: *Is it possible for a person to claim to be a Christian without actually knowing Christ? Could a large number of people really be completely ignorant of their own spiritual state?*

I assure you the answer to those questions is yes. You don't have to take my word for it. Instead, listen to the words of Jesus:

> **Not everyone who says to me, "Lord, Lord," will enter the kingdom of heaven, but only he who does the will of my Father who is in heaven. Many will say to me on that day, "Lord, Lord, did we not prophesy in your name, and in your name drive out demons and perform many miracles?" Then I will tell them plainly, "I never knew you. Away from me, you evildoers!"**
> **Matthew 7:21-23**

How do these verses impact you? Why?

All people are prone to spiritual deception, including you and me. What we need to understand is that Jesus wasn't speaking about outsiders in Matthew 7. He wasn't talking about atheists, murderers, or people who've completely rebelled against the message of the gospel. No, He was talking about religious people. He was talking about good people who superficially associate themselves with Him and do good things—even to the point of driving out demons and performing miracles. But they don't know Jesus.

What kinds of activities does our culture typically associate with Christian behavior and practices?

It's possible to go through the motions of a Christian life without actually becoming a Christian—without experiencing salvation. That should scare us on a number of different levels.

Let's address this problem by focusing on a genuine relationship with Christ—on what happens when people really experience salvation. What does it look like when people die to themselves and find new life as followers of Jesus? What evidence follows that spiritual transaction?

We can answer those questions by examining the experiences of Jesus' first disciples. When we do, two words stand out: *repent* and *renounce*.

Repent

We've already seen the way Jesus called His first disciples in Matthew 4:18-22. But if we back up to the previous verse, we see the first words of Jesus' public ministry on earth: "From that time on Jesus began to preach, 'Repent, for the kingdom of heaven is near' " (Matt. 4:17).

It's interesting that the very first word out of Jesus' mouth during His public ministry was *repent*. The same was true of John the Baptist, and Peter preached a message of repentance during the first Christian sermon after being filled with the Holy Spirit at Pentecost.

What ideas or images come to mind when you hear the word *repent*? Why?

Read the following passages and record what they teach about repentance.

Matthew 3:1-12

Acts 2:36-41

Repentance is a rich biblical term that signifies an elemental transformation in someone's mind, heart, and life. When people repent, they turn from walking in one direction to running in the opposite direction. From that point forward they think differently, believe differently, feel differently, love differently, and live differently.

How has your life changed as a result of following Jesus?

Have you consciously repented of your rebellion against God? Explain.

Fundamentally, repentance involves renouncing a former way of life in favor of a new way of life.

Renounce

Dictionary definitions of the word *renounce* include "to give up or put aside voluntarily" and "to repudiate; disown."[1] To renounce something is to commit a strong, decisive action. The term carries the weight of finality. That's precisely what Jesus wanted to communicate when He spoke these words to His disciples: "Any one of you who does not renounce all that he has cannot be my disciple" (Luke 14:33, ESV).

Contrary to what many believe today, Jesus wasn't speaking metaphorically or exaggerating when He made that statement. He meant what He said: that in order to follow Him, we must voluntarily relinquish control over every aspect of our lives. That includes our possessions, our comfort, our careers, our family, our position, our sin, and even ourselves.

That's what Jesus asked of His first disciples, and He asks the same of us today.

Look again at Matthew 4:18-22. Record three things Peter, Andrew, James, and John renounced in order to follow Jesus.

1.

2.

3.

Some people in the church are selling the notion that being a Christian means making a decision or praying a prayer and then retaining all of the details, priorities, and activities you've always known. Don't buy such a notion. Don't believe such a lie.

To become a Christian is to lose your life as you know it—to deny yourself, take up a cross, and follow Jesus. And to follow Jesus is to value what He values, go where He commands you to go, and do what He commands you to do. These are some of the most basic evidences of living as a disciple of Jesus.

Where do you see these basic forms of evidence reflected in your life?

What have you renounced as a result of following Jesus?

Tomorrow we'll look at an absolute must when it comes to following Jesus:

SOMETHING I REFER TO AS

SUPERNATURAL REGENERATION.

A NEW CREATION

On a recent trip to India, I had the opportunity to work with four different religious communities over a period of several days. It was an eye-opening experience, to say the least. I remember standing at the Ganges River, considered a holy body of water by Hindus. I watched as crowds of people washed themselves in the river to cleanse their sins. I observed individuals scattering the ashes of loved ones into the water, believing this ritual ensures instant salvation.

I remember listening in another region as Muslim calls to prayer resounded from loudspeakers five times each day. The people responded by filing into mosques and completing a series of prayers that involved bowing down with their hands on their knees, prostrating their faces to the ground, and then rising to stand.

I remember visiting a training center for Tibetan Buddhists where more than five hundred monks live together in the presence of two large temples. Everywhere I looked, I saw people bowing before statues of gold, walking in circles to recite mantras, and spinning prayer wheels.

I remember visiting a Sikh community during our final evening in India. Forbidden to cut their hair, men wore turbans of different colors, and women covered their heads. I watched as people entered their temple and bowed before the Sikh scriptures, known as the Guru Granth Sahib.

What experiences have you had with religious systems other than Christianity?

What do you think is the primary difference between Christianity and other religions?

Looking back on these four encounters with four major world religions, I realized they all shared one common denominator: in every religion a teacher (or a series of teachers) prescribes certain paths to follow in order to honor God (or different gods) and experience salvation (in whatever way that's defined).

In Hinduism ancient teachers have passed down Vedic traditions prescribing rites and rituals for Hindus to observe. In Islam Muhammad pointed to Five Pillars in the Qur'an for Muslims to practice. In Buddhism the Buddha's Eightfold Path is just one of Four Noble Truths he taught, alongside hundreds of other rules for Buddhists to follow. In Sikhism 10 gurus have pointed to one body of teaching as the way to truth and life.

Christianity is radically different from every other religious system in the world. And the root of that difference is a total rejection of superficial religion in the place of supernatural regeneration. We must understand this difference in order to be genuine disciples of Jesus Christ.

Superficial Religion

Christianity stands alone among world religions because when Jesus came on the scene of human history and began calling followers to Himself, He didn't say, "Follow certain rules. Observe specific regulations. Perform ritual duties. Pursue a particular path."

No. He said, "Follow Me."

With those two simple words Jesus made clear that His primary purpose wasn't to instruct His disciples in a prescribed religion. Rather, His purpose was to invite His disciples into a personal relationship. He wasn't saying, "Go this way to find truth and life." Instead, He was saying, "I am the way and the truth and the life" (John 14:6). The call of Jesus was "Come to *Me*. Find rest for your souls in *Me*. Find joy in your heart from *Me*. Find meaning in your life through *Me*."

This extremely shocking and utterly revolutionary call is the essence of what it means to be a disciple of Jesus. We aren't called to simply believe certain points or observe certain practices but to cling to the Person of Christ as life itself.

What's your reaction to the previous statements? Why?

Do you feel personally connected to Jesus? Why or why not?

I'm afraid the modern church has missed this distinction. In many ways and in many settings, we've relegated Christianity to just another choice in the cafeteria line of religions. Hindus bathe in the Ganges River; Christians get baptized in the church. Muslims go to worship on Friday; Christians go to worship on Sunday. Buddhists recite mantras; Christians sing choruses. Sikhs read their holy book and share with the needy; Christians read their Bibles and give to the poor.

Please don't misunderstand me: I'm definitely not saying Christians should avoid being baptized, singing in worship, reading our Bibles, or serving the poor. What I'm saying is that if we're not careful, any one of us could do all of these things completely apart from Jesus. Slowly and subtly we can allow Christianity to devolve into just another set of rules, regulations, practices, and principles—just another superficial religion.

How have you been led to follow rules and regulations as a church member?

Do you ever feel that your Christianity consists of nothing more than a list of truths to believe and things to do? Quiet times, prayer times, Bible study, small groups, service, evangelism—in the middle of it all, do you feel as if following Jesus is mostly duty with only a minimal amount of delight?

How do you answer the previous questions?

The curse of superficial religion is the constant pressure to do outward things apart from inward transformation, and it's exhausting. I know it's exhausting. More importantly, Jesus knows it's exhausting. And He invites us to something better:

> **Come to me, all you who are weary and burdened, and I will give you rest. Take my yoke upon you and learn from me, for I am gentle and humble in heart, and you will find rest for your souls. For my yoke is easy and my burden is light. Matthew 11:28-30**

What emotions did you experience when you read these verses? Why?

We live in a world where every other religious teacher says, "Try harder, work harder, do more, become better." But not Jesus. He offers a burden that's light. He offers rest. But the only way we can receive that rest is to reject superficial religion and instead look to God for the work of supernatural regeneration.

Supernatural Regeneration

If anyone understood the rigors and pressures of superficial religion, it was Nicodemus. Trained as a teacher of the law and a ruler among God's people, Nicodemus was like many professing Christians today: he possessed a measure of belief in and respect for Jesus while ordering his life around the commands of Scripture. He prayed and went to worship. He read and taught the Bible. He lived a good, decent, moral life.

For Nicodemus, everything was right on the outside, but something was wrong on the inside. Despite all the religious stuff he did, he had no spiritual life; he was empty. Fortunately, he came to Jesus seeking that spiritual life.

Jesus' answer to Nicodemus's questions was puzzling at first. He said, "I tell you the truth, no one can see the kingdom of God unless he is born again" (John 3:3). Jesus elaborated a couple of verses later, saying, "I tell you the truth, no one can enter the kingdom of God unless he is born of water and the Spirit (v. 5).

What images or ideas come to mind when you hear the phrase *born again?* Why?

NEW WAY TO WALK WITH JESUS –

That phrase "born of water and the Spirit" is key to understanding what Jesus was saying because it points back to an important passage from the Old Testament:

> **I will sprinkle clean water on you, and you will be clean; I will cleanse you from all your impurities and from all your idols. I will give you a new heart and put a new spirit in you; I will remove from you your heart of stone and give you a heart of flesh. And I will put my Spirit in you and move you to follow my decrees and be careful to keep my laws. Ezekiel 36:25-27**

What images or phrases strike you as most interesting in these verses? Why?

How do these verses connect with Jesus' words to Nicodemus?

What Ezekiel wrote about is exactly what Jesus came to do. He came to cleanse us of our sin through His sacrifice on the cross; to wash us with "clean water" (v. 25). And in doing so, He gives us something infinitely more valuable: a new heart. We're born again! He gives us His Spirit to live in us and change us from the inside out. This is what it means to experience supernatural regeneration.

That's why Paul wrote these joyful, exuberant words in 2 Corinthians 5:17: "If anyone is in Christ, he is a new creation; the old has gone, the new has come!"

That's also why the Bible teaches that faith alone in Christ alone is the only way to experience salvation from sin. Faith is the antiwork. It's the realization that we can do nothing to help ourselves except trust in what Jesus has done for us through His life, death, and resurrection.

Have you experienced supernatural regeneration? How can you tell?

Spiritual regeneration is the heart of Jesus' call to follow Him. When you become a Christian, you die, and Jesus becomes your life. To paraphrase Paul, "You have died with Christ, and you're not even alive anymore. Instead, Christ is alive in you, and the only way you live is by faith in Him" (Gal. 2:20, author's paraphrase). In other words, Jesus died for you so that He could live in you.

JESUS DOESN'T MERELY IMPROVE YOUR OLD NATURE; HE IMPARTS TO YOU AN ENTIRELY NEW NATURE—A SPIRITUAL NATURE THAT'S COMPLETELY UNITED WITH HIS.

MAKE DISCIPLES

Throughout this week we've explored what it means to be a disciple of Jesus Christ. We've looked at several pieces of evidence we can use to confirm whether we're truly following Jesus rather than going through the motions of cultural Christianity.

For example, we've seen that repentance is a vital first step for all Christians—leaving the path of rebellion against God and choosing instead to follow Christ. In addition, disciples of Jesus must renounce their comfort, careers, possessions, families, and even themselves. We've also seen that genuine Christians have experienced supernatural regeneration; they're changed from the inside out rather than settling for superficial beliefs and behaviors.

Today I want to explore the final proof of what it means to live as a genuine follower of Jesus: the reality that true disciples of Christ are supernaturally compelled to make more disciples of Christ.

Fishers of Men

Over the years I've been privileged to encounter many people in many places who've rejected the superficial religion of their culture and experienced supernatural regeneration through Christ. It's wonderful to hear their stories and see God's faithfulness win out over and over again.

For example, I often think of Abid, a doctor who lives on the most unevangelized island on earth. Abid came from a very wealthy, extremely devout Muslim family. He made a holy pilgrimage to Mecca seven different times as part of his attempts to find meaning in life through Islam. But by God's grace Abid encountered Christian missionaries who shared the gospel with him. As he heard about Christ, Abid experienced a peace that had eluded him throughout his entire life in Islam. Eventually he became a follower of Jesus.

The cost was steep. As soon as his family found out about his conversion, Abid was tied up and beaten. His wife left him, his kids abandoned him, he lost his medical practice, and today he lives under a constant threat of death from his extended family.

But those difficulties aren't what occupies Abid's mind. Instead, he thinks about helping others find the joy and purpose he's been blessed to receive. When he was saved, Abid asked God to use him to share the gospel with one thousand people during his first year as a Christian. At the end of that first year, God had given him the opportunity to share the good news of His grace in Christ with more than four thousand people.

Abid still experiences persecution, but he presses forward. Indeed, it seems as though nothing can stop him from making disciples.

Abid's experiences are a continuation of Jesus' call to His first disciples in Matthew 4. This is true not simply because Abid is working to make disciples but because his work is a result of being profoundly changed by Jesus Christ.

Look again at Jesus' words to those first disciples: " 'Come, follow me,' Jesus said, 'and *I will make you* fishers of men' " (Matt. 4:19, emphasis added). Notice Jesus didn't say He would *call* them to be fishers of men; He didn't say He would instruct the disciples in techniques for evangelism or serve as a role model. No, He said He would *cause* them to be fishers of men. The commands He would give *to* them could be accomplished only by the work He would do *in* them.

And that's what happened. In the years that followed, Jesus transformed everything about the disciples' lives: their thoughts, their desires, their wills, their relationships, and ultimately their very purpose for living. Not surprisingly, the Book of Matthew ends with Jesus' command for His disciples to make more disciples—what we know as the Great Commission:

> **Jesus came to them and said, "All authority in heaven and on earth has been given to me. Therefore go and make disciples of all nations, baptizing them in the name of the Father and of the Son and of the Holy Spirit, and teaching them to obey everything I have commanded you. And surely I am with you always, to the very end of the age." Matthew 28:18-20**

What are your initial reactions to Jesus' words in these verses?

Do Jesus' commands in these verses apply to you? Why or why not?

Moving Forward?

Considering Jesus' call makes me wonder what we're missing now. When I look at the church today, it seems that we've taken the costly command of Christ to go, baptize, and teach all nations and mutated it into a comfortable call for people to come, be baptized, and sit in one location. Many Christians seem to have exempted themselves from any personal responsibility to fish for men, and I'm convinced the majority of Christians wouldn't identify making disciples of all nations as their primary purpose in life.

What's your reaction to the previous statements?

Is making disciples of all nations the primary goal for your life? What evidence supports your answer?

If you feel offended or shamed by these ideas, please stay with me. Those of us in the church must understand that biblically speaking, every disciple of Jesus is intended to make more disciples of Jesus. From the very beginning of Christianity, following Jesus has always involved fishing for men.

What's more, those early disciples didn't have to be coaxed into making more disciples. They didn't evangelize from a sense of guilt or duty. Instead, they were supernaturally compelled. Not even the threat of death could stop them from obeying Jesus' command.

Think of Peter and John in the days after the launch of the church at Pentecost. In a seemingly random encounter they healed a crippled beggar at a temple gate (see Acts 3:1-10). When that action created a stir throughout Jerusalem, the religious leaders arrested and interrogated Peter and John (see Acts 4:1-7).

Read Acts 4:8-20 to see what happened next. What words would you use to summarize Peter's actions and proclamations?

Has there been a time when you couldn't help speaking about what you'd seen and heard about Jesus? Explain.

So what's keeping us from obeying that command today? Not the church as a whole but every individual Christian. Why are so many of us sitting on the sidelines instead of wholeheartedly, passionately, sacrificially, and joyfully giving our lives to make disciples of all nations?

What's preventing you from giving more of your life to make disciples of all nations?

I think the answer is tied to what we discussed yesterday: superficial religion. If our Christianity is nothing more than a list of principles to believe and practices to observe—many of which are similar to the principles and practices of other religions—then we'll always view making disciples as a duty. It will always be a chore, and we'll have little or no motivation to step out of our comfort zones, alter our priorities, sacrifice our possessions, and potentially even lose our lives to share Christ with others. As Jesus said, "No one can serve two masters. Either he will hate the one and love the other, or he will be devoted to the one and despise the other" (Matt. 6:24).

If we've experienced supernatural regeneration, on the other hand—if the God of the universe has stretched His hand of mercy into the depths of our souls, forgiven all our sin, and filled us with His Spirit—then such a spectator mentality is spiritually impossible. For people whose hearts, minds, wills, and relationships have been radically turned upside down by the Person of Christ, the purpose of Christ will reign supreme.

What about you? Are you engulfed in superficial religion, or have you experienced supernatural regeneration? Are you concentrating on Christian principles and practices in your life, or are you clinging to Christ as your very life? Are you confident that you've been forgiven of your sin? Is it clear that you're filled with His Spirit?

Ultimately, have you been born again?

How do you answer the previous question?

Are you currently compelled to make disciples of Jesus Christ? Are you succeeding?

" 'Follow me,' Jesus said, 'and I will make you fishers of men' " (Matt. 4:19). This isn't a gentle solicitation to tread a path of superficial religion. It's a call to taste a pleasure that can be found only in a supernatural relationship with Christ.

WILL YOU FOLLOW?

1. "Renounce," *Dictionary.com* [online, cited 28 November 2012]. Available from the Internet: *www.dictionary.reference.com*.

WEEK 2
BE TRANSFORMED

Welcome back to this group discussion of *Follow Me*.

Last week's application activity involved praying daily for the salvation of five specific people. If you're comfortable, share ways those prayers affected the rest of your daily routine.

Describe what you liked best about the study material in week 1. What questions do you have?

What ideas or images come to mind when you hear words like *Lord* and *King*? Why?

How have you changed since becoming a follower of Jesus? Record three of the biggest changes you've personally experienced since choosing to follow Christ.

1.

2.

3.

To prepare to view the DVD segment, read aloud John 15:5-8:

> **I am the vine; you are the branches. If a man remains in me and I in him, he will bear much fruit; apart from me you can do nothing. If anyone does not remain in me, he is like a branch that is thrown away and withers; such branches are picked up, thrown into the fire and burned. If you remain in me and my words remain in you, ask whatever you wish, and it will be given you. This is to my Father's glory, that you bear much fruit, showing yourselves to be my disciples.**

WATCH

Complete the viewer guide below as you watch DVD session 2.

As a disciple of Christ, you are _____ with Christ.

As a Christian, Christ is _____ you.

You are in _____.

Christ is _____ you.

You are with _____.

When you _____ Jesus as Lord,
   He changes everything in your life.

As we abide in His Word, we bear
   _____ in this world.

God's Word _____ us.

God's Word _____ us.

God's Word _____ us.

God's Word _____ us.

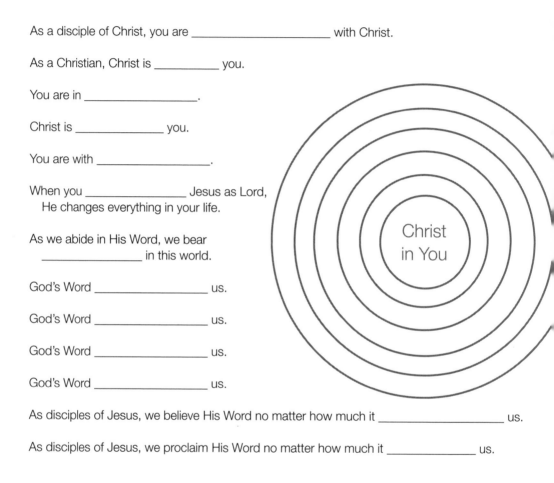

As disciples of Jesus, we believe His Word no matter how much it _____ us.

As disciples of Jesus, we proclaim His Word no matter how much it _____ us.

Video sessions available for purchase at *www.lifeway.com/followme*

Discuss the DVD segment with your group, using the questions below.

What did you like best from David's teaching? Why?

Review the three ways you've changed since becoming a follower of Christ, which you listed earlier in this group session. Where do those changes fit into the concentric-circles diagram shown on the left?

Why is it important that Jesus transforms us from the inside out?

Respond to David's statement: "This is what it means to be a disciple of Jesus: it means that He is in you, Jesus is in you, and you are in Him. He is with you every moment of every day, forever, and you are with Him in His life and His death and His resurrection and His reign."

How has your purpose in life changed as a result of following Jesus?

Describe your level of satisfaction with your efforts to study God's Word. What obstacles currently hinder you from a deeper study of the Scriptures?

What are some appropriate ways to proclaim the truths of God's Word in today's culture?

Application: Identify one of your favorite chapters from the Bible and commit to read it every day this week. Suggestions include Matthew 5; Romans 8; Romans 12; and James 3. Conclude each reading by asking yourself, *Does the way I live my life indicate that I believe what these verses say?*

Scripture: Memorize John 15:5 this week.

READ week 2 and complete the activities before the next group experience.
READ chapters 3–4 in the book *Follow Me* by David Platt (Tyndale, 2013).

This Week's Scripture Memory

I am the vine; you are the branches. If a man remains in me and I in him, he will bear much fruit; apart from me you can do nothing. John 15:5

Many things in modern society are customizable; they can be twisted, tweaked, shaped, and adapted to fit our personal desires. If I buy a new car, for example, I can pick and choose from a variety of different options so that I can have a car that does all of the things I want it to do. If I order a meal at a restaurant, I can typically have the ingredients for that meal adjusted to fit my personal preferences.

Such customization is often helpful and provides many benefits for many stations of life. Unfortunately, many of us have wrongly attempted to apply the principle of customization when it comes to following Jesus. Often without realizing it, we have a tendency to redefine Christianity according to our own tastes, preferences, church traditions, and cultural norms.

Slowly, subtly, we take the Jesus of the Bible and twist Him into someone with whom we're a little more comfortable. We dilute what He said about the cost of following Him, disregard what He said about those who choose not to follow Him, misread what He said about materialism, and functionally miss what He said about mission. We pick and choose what we like and don't like from Jesus' teachings and in the end create a nice, nonoffensive, politically correct, middle-class, American Jesus who looks and thinks just like us.

Here's the problem: Jesus isn't customizable. He hasn't left Himself open to interpretation, adaptation, innovation, or alteration. He's spoken clearly through His Word, and we have no right to conform Him to our own lives and our own desires.

Quite the contrary. To follow Christ is to be conformed to *His* image as He transforms our minds and wills through His truth. We bend to Him. We adapt to Him. Ultimately, we submit to Him as Lord.

BE TRANSFORMED

UNITED WITH CHRIST

A large number of images and symbols have been connected with Christianity in the centuries since Jesus called His first disciples and launched what we know today as the church. The cross is the most common example. Millions of people display a replica of that instrument of torture in their homes or wear it around their necks to identify with Jesus' crucifixion.

The *ichthys* is another common example—what many people today refer to as the Jesus fish. In the early church, believers used the *ichthys* to mark meeting places without drawing unwanted attention from the Jewish and Roman authorities. The fish was also used as a way to identify potential believers. When a believer met a stranger on the road, for example, he often drew the first arch of the *ichthys* in the sand; if the stranger completed the drawing, the believer knew he was in good company.[1] (Apparently, this was the ancient equivalent of gluing a Jesus fish to the back of your car.)

What other images and symbols are regularly connected with Christianity?

How have images and symbols contributed to your Christian education?

Today we're going to study a powerful image Jesus used to help His followers understand what it means to serve Him as Lord.

Vines and Branches

One of the reasons Jesus was such a great teacher is that He commonly used object lessons and illustrations that were near at hand. As He and the disciples walked together through a field or a city, Jesus would point out something right in front of the disciples that perfectly illustrated what He was teaching.

Read the following passages of Scripture and record what Jesus communicated through each object lesson.

Matthew 6:28-30

Mark 4:21-23

Luke 13:18-21

One of Jesus' most important object lessons is recorded in John 15, where He referred to a vine and its branches as a way to understand what it means to truly follow Him as a disciple:

> **I am the vine; you are the branches. If a man remains in me and I in him, he will bear much fruit; apart from me you can do nothing. If anyone does not remain in me, he is like a branch that is thrown away and withers; such branches are picked up, thrown into the fire and burned. If you remain in me and my words remain in you, ask whatever you wish, and it will be given you. This is to my Father's glory, that you bear much fruit, showing yourselves to be my disciples. John 15:5-8**

What encourages you most in this passage? Why?

What do you find most challenging about these verses? Why?

I hope you feel the shocking intimacy of Jesus' words in this passage. When we consider what it means to follow Jesus, we typically think in terms of His leading us where He wants us to go. We think of Jesus out in front and us following behind. In our mind's eye there's always a gap between us and Christ—a separation.

But that's not the idea Jesus communicated in John 15. Instead, His reference to a vine and its branches is a powerful image evoking deep connection. According to these verses, we're connected with Jesus as intimately as branches are connected to the tree from which they grow. All we are—life, thoughts, actions—grows from this connection with Christ. All of our physical, emotional, and spiritual needs are supplied through our relationship with Him.

What's your reaction to the previous statements? Why?

Jesus wanted His present and future disciples to understand that following Him involves more than intellectual agreement—even more than obedience and faith. Rather, followers of Jesus are united to their Lord in a supernatural and life-giving way.

A Primary Theme

These ideas aren't limited to this single illustration in John 15. In fact, the New Testament describes a Christian's unity with Christ from a number of different angles and through a number of different authors.

A little earlier in John 14, for example, Jesus began preparing the disciples for His coming death and eventual departure from this world. He told them, "I will not leave you as orphans; I will come to you. On that day you will realize that I am in my Father, and you are in me, *and I am in you*" (vv. 18,20, emphasis added). In Galatians 2 Paul wrote, "I have been crucified with Christ and I no longer live, but *Christ lives in me.* The life I live in the body, I live by faith in the Son of God, who loved me and gave himself for me" (v. 20, emphasis added).

It's wonderful to hear Jesus say, "I will come to you" and that He "gave himself" for us. But it's shocking to hear Him say, "I am in you" and that Christ lives in me. To be a Christian is to experience an intimate connection with Jesus—to have Him live inside you. Believers are incredibly blessed in this way.

In your own words, what does it mean that Christ is in you?

Not only does the Bible emphasize Christ in us, but it also teaches over and over that we as Christians are in Christ. We share in His experiences just as He shares in our lives.

Read the following passages of Scripture and record what they teach about Christians being in Christ.

2 Corinthians 5:17

Ephesians 1:3-4

Philippians 4:7

Jesus also emphasized our intimate connection with Him in one of the most famous passages in Scripture (and some of His last words to the disciples)—the Great Commission:

> **All authority in heaven and on earth has been given to me. Therefore go and make disciples of all nations, baptizing them in the name of the Father and of the Son and of the Holy Spirit, and teaching them to obey everything I have commanded you. *And surely I am with you always, to the very end of the age.* Matthew 28:18-20, emphasis added**

What do you find most challenging about these verses? Why?

When have you experienced strength or support from your connection with Jesus?

The Bible says Christ is inside us and we're inside Christ. It says Christ is with us. And finally, the Bible says we're *with* Christ.

In Romans 6:5-8 Paul wrote that we as Christians are crucified with Christ, buried with Christ, and resurrected with Christ. In Ephesians 2 Paul wrote that "God, who is rich in mercy, made us alive with Christ even when we were dead in transgressions" (vv. 4-5). First Corinthians 1:9 says God "has called you into fellowship with his Son Jesus Christ."

If you're a Christian, please feel the weight and wonder of these things. Let the reality soak in that living as a disciple of Jesus doesn't mean following Him as a dog follows its master. No! To follow Jesus means to be supernaturally connected with Him and with all He represents.

If you're a Christian, Jesus Christ lives in you and is with you. Moreover, you live in Jesus and are with Him. That's what He meant in John 15:4 when He told His disciples to "remain in me, and I will remain in you."

TO BE A CHRISTIAN IS TO EXPERIENCE UNITY WITH CHRIST.

JESUS CHANGES EVERYTHING

The world we live in is filled with contrasts. Think about the differences between day and night, for example. Think of holding something hot in one hand and something cold in the other. Think of encountering the roar of an engine after listening to a gentle breeze.

Contrasts are all around us, but we feel them more deeply when they have more of an impact on our lives. The contrast between wealth and poverty always takes center stage in world events, for instance, because it impacts so many facets of our culture and our individual experiences.

Life and Death

The most striking contrast of all has to be the difference between life and death—between things that possess vitality and energy and things that are cold, unfeeling, and inert.

That's the contrast Jesus wanted to emphasize early in John 15:

> **I am the true vine, and my Father is the gardener. He cuts off every branch in me that bears no fruit, while every branch that does bear fruit he prunes so that it will be even more fruitful. You are already clean because of the word I have spoken to you. Remain in me, and I will remain in you. No branch can bear fruit by itself; it must remain in the vine. Neither can you bear fruit unless you remain in me. I am the vine; you are the branches. If a man remains in me and I in him, he will bear much fruit; apart from me you can do nothing. John 15:1-5**

What images stand out to you in these verses? Why?

In your own words, what do those images represent?

A branch that's lying on the ground has a very different experience from a branch that's still connected to the vine. Branches on the ground are dead. They receive no nutrients, and they have no hope of future growth. They're fruitless. As a result, their only value is to be collected and burned. Branches that are still connected to the vine are vastly different because they have life. They receive life-giving nutrients from the vine, which means they're able to produce more life in the form of fruit. They have energy and purpose.

The point of Jesus' imagery in John 15 is that those who follow Him are spiritually alive only because of Him. We've been blessed with a life-giving connection, and we must realize that our union with Christ is the sole source of our energy, purpose, and success. That's why Paul wrote these words: "Do not offer the parts of your body to sin, as instruments of wickedness, but rather offer yourselves to God, as those who have been brought from death to life" (Rom. 6:13).

In what ways do you express your gratitude to Jesus for granting you this life-giving connection?

What obstacles prevent you from expressing gratitude to Jesus? How can these obstacles be overcome?

As Christians, we experience unity with Christ, and the immediate result of that unity is life; it's a spiritual resurrection. But there's more. When we follow Jesus as Lord, He also transforms us from the inside out.

Jesus Transforms Our Thoughts

Last week we explored the concept of supernatural regeneration: that by being born again, we become followers of Christ and new creations by the power of the Holy Spirit. Using the imagery of John 15, we can say that this moment of supernatural regeneration is the moment we become connected with Jesus as the Vine.

But what happens next? Do we instantly become perfect as a result of that connection? Do we see all of our problems solved and begin living as Jesus would in every facet of our lives? Obviously not. As Christians, we still struggle with sin and doubt, trials and rebellion.

Yet we're not the same as we once were. When we're attached to the Vine, Jesus lives in us and is with us; we live in Him and are with Him. As a result, from the moment we accept Jesus' call to follow Him, He begins to transform everything about us from the inside out.

In what ways have you experienced transformation as a result of following Jesus?

First, when we're united with Christ, He begins to transform our thoughts. He changes the way we perceive and process information so that, over time, we're able to think more and more like Him. Paul wrote about this transformation in 1 Corinthians 2:

> **We have not received the spirit of the world but the Spirit who is from God, that we may understand what God has freely given us. This is what we speak, not in words taught us by human wisdom but in words taught by the Spirit, expressing spiritual truths in spiritual words. The man without the Spirit does not accept the things that come from the Spirit of God, for they are foolishness to him, and he cannot understand them, because they are spiritually discerned. 1 Corinthians 2:12-14**

Read 1 Corinthians 2:16. What does it mean when it says "we have the mind of Christ"?

Paul also wrote about the benefits of this transformation:

> **Do not conform any longer to the pattern of this world, but be transformed by the renewing of your mind. Then you will be able to test and approve what God's will is—his good, pleasing and perfect will. Romans 12:2**

By renewing our minds, God prevents us from being conformed to the sinful pattern of this world. Even better, our transformed thoughts enable us to connect with and confirm God's will—something we'll explore in greater detail tomorrow.

Don't overlook the importance of these truths. When Jesus transforms what we think, He also transforms what we believe. And as He transforms our core beliefs, we begin to separate from the world and live instead as members of God's kingdom.

In what ways should Christians think differently than people in the world who don't know Christ?

Jesus Transforms Our Desires

In the same way, Jesus transforms our desires. He renovates our feelings and affections—what we long for and struggle to achieve. As you can imagine, that's huge in a society such as ours that's built on continual consumption as a way to fulfill worldly desires.

This issue of desire is important because it exposes a fundamental flaw in the way we view ourselves as Western Christians. When we think of sinful desires, we tend to picture extremes. We think of adultery and murder. We think of the extreme greed demonstrated by big-corporation CEOs. We think of primitive tribes worshiping false gods in a foreign land.

But what about our Western obsession with lust and pornography? What about the hours we spend day in and day out glued to ungodly movies and television shows? What about our continual shopping for more and more possessions? What about our fanatical desire to look better than those around us? What about our busy efforts to climb the corporate ladder? What about our incessant worship of sports, food, celebrity gossip, and other worldly indulgences?

All of these are sinful desires, and they inevitably lead us to false worship—to idolatry.

What's your reaction to the previous statement? Why?

How can we identify when our desires are leading us to false worship? What are the symptoms of that reality?

What steps can we take to turn away from idolatry?

"No one can serve two masters. Either he will hate the one and love the other, or he will be devoted to the one and despise the other" (Matt. 6:24). Jesus spoke these words to specifically combat the love of money, but they apply equally well to any false desire that threatens to twist our affections.

We move past these false desires only when Jesus transforms our affections. We begin to hate the things of this earth that we once loved. More importantly, we begin to love the things of God that we once hated.

THIS IS AN IMPORTANT BENEFIT OF CHOOSING TO FOLLOW HIM.

FROM INTERNAL TO EXTERNAL

If you're like most people, you don't enjoy being sick. And if you're like most people, myself included, you typically think of illnesses in terms of the external symptoms they produce.

When you catch a cold, for example, you primarily view it in terms of the runny nose, the sneezing, the itchy eyes, and so on. You think of the way your brain seems to fog up when you take too much cold medicine. You think of how annoying it is to miss work or suffer through your job in a less productive state. All of these are external symptoms.

What's interesting is that most illnesses have more to do with what's going on internally than externally. Sure, there are a few instances when sickness works from the outside in—an infection or a bite from a poisonous animal, for example. But those are rare.

Most of our illnesses start on the inside and then work themselves out as external symptoms. Maybe colonies of bacteria multiply in your bloodstream or digestive tract. Maybe hordes of viruses attack your cells and turn them into factories that produce more and more viruses. Maybe you eat something that doesn't agree with you.

Whatever the specifics may be, illnesses almost always affect us from the inside out.

What was the last illness you contracted? What were the main symptoms of that illness?

What was the root cause of that illness?

On a much more positive note, a similar movement's at play in the Christian life—a progression from internal change toward the external symptoms of that change. As we explored in yesterday's material, people become connected with Jesus when they answer the call to follow Him as Lord. And through that connection, Jesus actively transforms us from the inside out.

Jesus begins this transformation with our minds and also moves to renovate our desires. These are internal matters. Before long, however, His transforming work begins to impact us externally as He changes our will, our relationships, and the very purpose of our lives.

Jesus Transforms Our Will

Once we begin to think the way Jesus thinks and desire what Jesus desires, it's only a matter of time before we start acting the way Jesus acts—before we start living according to His will instead of our own. As this transformation progresses, we sin less frequently and spend more time and resources investing in God's kingdom.

Using the language of John 15, we begin to "bear much fruit" (v. 5).

Unfortunately, many Christians have an inadequate or improper understanding of how Jesus transforms our wills and actions. In fact, many Christians actually block Jesus from doing His transforming work in their lives. That's because so many of us still rely on human wisdom and human willpower as the primary methods for combating sin.

What ideas or images come to mind when you hear the word *willpower*?

Do you feel that you possess a large amount of willpower? Why or why not?

Think of the many areas of impurity across the church and among Christians in our culture—pornography, adultery, gluttony, materialism, idolatry, greed, rage, drunkenness, and so on. When we give in to these temptations, we prove that we desire the fleeting, momentary pleasure of some fling or rush more than we desire the unfading, eternal pleasure of knowing, enjoying, and experiencing God.

Obviously, that's a problem. But we too often address these struggles and temptations by telling ourselves (and telling one another) to do better: *Stop doing that! Don't spend so much time online! Don't watch those shows! Stay away from bars! Sell some of your stuff! Get rid of your credit cards! Find an accountability partner!*

While there's nothing wrong with any of those statements, they're all based on human effort and human will. That's a problem because our struggles with sin are almost always rooted in areas where Christ has yet to transform our thoughts and desires. In other words, we're defeated when we try to adjust our actions before we've allowed Christ to adjust our minds and our desires.

What's your reaction to the previous statements? Why?

Read the following passages of Scripture and record the ways sinful actions resulted from misplaced thoughts and desires.

Genesis 3:1-7

2 Samuel 11:1-16

Acts 5:1-11

How do we combat sin in our lives? By trusting and allowing Christ to transform our thoughts and our desires—even more, by inviting Him to do so: "Jesus, I'm tempted to lust right now; please purify my heart and my mind." "Lord, I've been acquiring more and more stuff for months; please help me to think as You think and desire what You desire when it comes to possessions."

It's only through Jesus' transformational work that our wills become aligned with His will, and therefore our actions become aligned with His actions.

Where do you struggle most in terms of sinful actions?

What are the root thoughts and desires that produce those sinful actions?

Notice the incredible blessing we receive as a result of this process: "If you remain in me and my words remain in you, ask whatever you wish, and it will be given you" (John 15:7). At first blush these verses seem too good to be true. Indeed, all of us have had many experiences where God declined to fulfill our requests. So what did Jesus mean?

In truth, this verse offers the key to understanding prayer in the life of a Christian—but that key involves two steps. The first step is for us to make our wants the same as God's wants. That's what we've been talking about: the transformation of our will. As we remain in Christ and His Word, He transforms the way we think and what we desire. He changes our wants to match His.

Once that's happened, the second step is easy: we simply ask for whatever we want. And when our desires have been transformed to line up with God's desires—with God's will—He will grant our requests. He will give us what we want because it's the same as what He wants.

What's your reaction to the previous statements?

How do those statements impact your views of prayer? How will they impact the way you pray?

Jesus Transforms Our Relationships

As our transformation continues to progress from internal to external, Jesus impacts more than our individual actions. He also transforms our relationships with others. Specifically, He gives us the ability to love others as He loves them:

> **My command is this: Love each other as I have loved you. Greater love has no one than this, that he lay down his life for his friends. You are my friends if you do what I command. I no longer call you servants, because a servant does not know his master's business. Instead, I have called you friends, for everything that I learned from my Father I have made known to you. John 15:12-15**

Look at those first two words: "My command." Jesus didn't suggest Christians love one another even to the point of laying down their lives; He commanded it. And He repeated that command in verse 17, just in case we missed it the first time: "This is my command: Love each other."

As we abide in Christ and Christ abides in us, He transforms our ability to love and relate with others. He enables us to love our neighbors as ourselves (see Matt. 22:39). As a result, Christians should be distinguishable from the rest of the world because of our relationships with one another and with those who still need Christ:

> **A new command I give you: Love one another. As I have loved you, so you must love one another. By this all men will know that you are my disciples, if you love one another. John 13:34-35**

In what ways do you express sacrificial love for other Christians?

In what ways do you express sacrificial love for those who still need Christ?

Jesus Transforms Our Purpose

Abiding in Christ means being transformed from the inside out. It means losing our human thoughts, desires, wills, and relationships to gain the thoughts, desires, wills, and relationships of Jesus. Ultimately, abiding in Christ transforms the very purpose of our existence in the world.

As followers of Jesus, we don't strive to accomplish what people in the world strive for. We have a different purpose. Specifically, we're called to glorify God by producing fruit for His kingdom:

> **I am the vine; you are the branches. If a man remains in me and I in him, he will bear much fruit; apart from me you can do nothing. John 15:5**
>
> **You did not choose me, but I chose you and appointed you to go and bear fruit—fruit that will last. Then the Father will give you whatever you ask in my name. John 15:16**

In what ways are you currently producing fruit for God's kingdom?

What obstacles are preventing you from producing more fruit? How can they be overcome?

To follow Jesus is to be transformed from the inside out. The way you think becomes totally different from the rest of the world. What you desire becomes different from the rest of the world.

YOUR WILL, YOUR RELATIONSHIPS, EVEN YOUR ENTIRE

PURPOSE FOR LIVING IS TURNED UPSIDE DOWN

AS YOU ABIDE IN JESUS AND AS HE ABIDES IN YOU.

ABIDE IN GOD'S WORD

With many things in life there's a big difference between intellectual knowledge and practical knowledge—between experiences based on understanding and experiences based on doing.

It's one thing to understand the rules of football, for example, but it's quite another thing to put on a helmet and try to push a three-hundred-pound man around the field. That would be an experience based on doing. In the same way, reading a recipe for Key lime pie can be an intellectual experience, but actually working through the process to create something edible requires a certain amount of practical knowledge.

These differences often apply to theological concepts, as well. For example, all week we've been exploring the idea of remaining or abiding in Christ. But what does that mean? We can get an intellectual understanding of the concept by reflecting on the imagery of ourselves as branches connected to Christ as the Vine, but such an understanding doesn't translate well to our everyday routines.

Speaking practically, what part do we play when it comes to remaining in Christ? What choices do we need to make in order to remain in Him? What actions do we need to take?

These are the questions we'll explore today.

Believe the Scriptures

One of the primary ways we practically remain in Jesus—if not the primary way—is by abiding in His Word. Jesus made that clear several times in John 15:

> You are already clean *because of the word I have spoken to you.* Remain in me, and I will remain in you. No branch can bear fruit by itself; it must remain in the vine. Neither can you bear fruit unless you remain in me. John 15:3-4, emphasis added

> If you remain in me and *my words remain in you,* ask whatever you wish, and it will be given you. John 15:7, emphasis added

What do you find most interesting about these verses? Why?

So part of what it means to remain in Jesus is to spend regular time reading the Bible, which is His Word. But we know from James that even the demons have an intellectual awareness of what God has revealed in His Word—and shudder (see Jas. 2:19).

Therefore, Jesus makes it clear that obedience is also part of the equation:

> **As the Father has loved me, so have I loved you. Now remain in my love. *If you obey my commands,* you will remain in my love, just as I have obeyed my Father's commands and remain in his love. John 15:9-10, emphasis added**

What are some commands Jesus has given us in His Word? Record three.

1.

2.

3.

To remain connected with Christ and experience His transformation, we must continually encounter His Word. We must read His Word in order to understand it, we must understand it in order to believe, and we must believe it in order to obey. What this really means on a practical basis is that we submit our lives to the Scriptures.

Maybe you object to that idea. Maybe part of you wonders, *Isn't it crazy for us to base our 21st-century lives on the words of a man from the 1st century? Aren't some of the Bible's teachings simply archaic? Haven't we experienced cultural developments and discovered scientific advancements since the days when Jesus lived?*

In other words, how do we know that what Jesus taught two thousand years ago is still true today?

What's your response to the previous question?

This is where we realize the authority of Jesus' words is tied to the reality of His resurrection. Think about it. If Jesus didn't rise from the dead, then ultimately we don't have to worry about anything He said. In that case He would be just like every other religious teacher in the world, teaching principles and imparting opinions for living a better life. In fact, He'd be far worse because of the promises He made. If Jesus wasn't resurrected, then all of Christianity is a hoax, and Christians are the most pitiably stupid people on the planet (see 1 Cor. 15:16-19).

But if Jesus rose from the dead—if He did what no one else in all of history has ever done or will ever do—then we can't just accept what Jesus said as good advice. We must alter everything in our lives to conform to His Word.

Do you believe Jesus rose from the dead and has spoken with supernatural authority through the Bible? Why or why not?

Does your everyday routine reflect your answer to the previous question? Explain.

Here's the good news: remaining in Jesus will give us satisfaction and joy in this life and beyond:

> **If you obey my commands, you will remain in my love, just as I have obeyed my Father's commands and remain in his love. I have told you this so that my joy may be in you and that your joy may be complete. John 15:10-11**

In what ways have you experienced joy as a follower of Christ?

Better still, remaining in Jesus allows us to develop a genuine friendship with the Creator of the universe.

Read John 15:12-16. What's your initial reaction to these verses?

Do you consider yourself to be a friend of Jesus? Why or why not?

The bad news, unfortunately, is that remaining in Jesus won't be easy in this world. There will be consequences.

Believe Through Consequences

There's no question about it: to follow Jesus and remain in Him is to live very differently from the rest of the world. In fact, by following Jesus, you'll often set yourself against the rest of the world.

You'll think differently about money and possessions, and the world will notice. You'll think differently about success and ambition, and the world will notice. You'll think differently about pleasure, time, and love, and the world will notice.

For all of these reasons and more, the world will hate you:

> If the world hates you, keep in mind that it hated me first. If you belonged to the world, it would love you as its own. As it is, you do not belong to the world, but I have chosen you out of the world. That is why the world hates you. Remember the words I spoke to you: "No servant is greater than his master." If they persecuted me, they will persecute you also. If they obeyed my teaching, they will obey yours also. They will treat you this way because of my name, for they do not know the One who sent me. John 15:18-21

What do these verses teach about Christians and persecution?

When have you felt persecuted by the world because of your decision to follow Christ?

In spite of our dissonance with the world, Jesus made it clear that His disciples must proclaim His Word:

> **When the Counselor comes, whom I will send to you from the Father, the Spirit of truth who goes out from the Father, he will testify about me. And you also must testify, for you have been with me from the beginning.**
> **John 15:26-27**

In what ways have you encountered "the Spirit of truth"?

How has the Holy Spirit helped you testify about Jesus and His gospel?

The call from Christ is clear: believe My Word, obey My Word, and proclaim My Word, even when it costs your life.

BEAR THE FRUIT OF THIS WORD IN THE WORLD,

EVEN IF THAT MEANS LOSING EVERYTHING ELSE.

PERSONAL DISCIPLE-MAKING PLAN: FILL YOUR MIND WITH TRUTH

I wrote earlier about the blessing my wife, Heather, and I experienced when we adopted our son Caleb from Kazakhstan. That was a joyful moment, but it was preceded by a long stretch of dark and difficult days. For years Heather and I had tried to have children biologically, but to no avail. When we became convinced it would never happen, we began the process of adopting Caleb.

Imagine my surprise, then, when Heather sat me down on our couch two weeks after returning home with Caleb and spoke those words I'd given up any chance of hearing: "I'm pregnant." I was shocked. Apparently, what happens in Kazakhstan doesn't stay in Kazakhstan!

What experiences have you had in connection with the birth of a baby?

What emotions do you feel when you reflect on those experiences?

Looking back on our years of infertility, Heather and I still remember the hurts and heartaches of longing to have children yet finding those longings unfulfilled with every passing month. We constantly felt the frustration that comes with realizing something was physically wrong that prevented this blessing.

In hindsight I'm convinced the Lord used those experiences to teach me an important lesson: that the same thing can be said of the Christian life. By God's design He's wired His children for spiritual reproduction. He's woven into the fabric of every single Christian's DNA a desire and an ability to reproduce. More than any couple longs to naturally reproduce, a Christian longs to see sinners supernaturally saved. All who know the love of Christ yearn to multiply the life of Christ. God has formed, fashioned, and even filled Christians with His Spirit for this very purpose.

Therefore, I think it's reasonable to conclude that something's spiritually amiss at the core of a Christian if his or her relationship with Christ doesn't result in reproduction. Maybe more plainly put, wherever you find a Christian who isn't leading men and women to Christ and helping them grow in their relationship with Christ, something is very wrong.

To be a disciple of Jesus is to make disciples of Jesus.

What's your reaction to the previous statements? Why?

Something's wrong in the lives of many Christians today. Somewhere along the way, we've tragically minimized what it means to be a follower of Jesus and virtually ignored the biblical expectation that we fish for men. The result is a rampant spectator mentality that skews disciple-ship across the church, stifles the spread of the gospel around the world, and ultimately sears the heart of what it means for each of us to be a Christian.

Tough Questions

So I must ask: Are you reproducing? Can you point to a man, woman, or child to whom you've specifically proclaimed the gospel message in recent months? Can you point to someone you're discipling because he or she responded to that proclamation?

How do you answer these questions?

Do you desire to reproduce spiritually? Deep down inside, do you long to see people come to know Christ through your life?

If you don't desire to reproduce and if you don't long to see people come to know Christ through your life, then I encourage you in the words of 2 Corinthians 13:5 to "examine [yourself] to see whether you are in the faith." Is Christ in you? And if He's not—if your heart, mind, and will haven't been transformed by the forgiveness of your sins and the filling of his Spirit—then I urge you to die to sin and yourself today and come to life in Christ.

What's your reaction to the previous statements? Why?

On the other hand, if you desire spiritual reproduction as a disciple of Jesus and if you long to see people come to know Christ through your life, I invite you to take some intentional steps toward that goal.

Every year I fill out what I call a Personal Disciple-Making Plan. Basically, it's my effort in God's grace to set out the way I want to wholeheartedly follow Christ and fish for men in the coming year. I ask each pastor in our church to go through the same process, along with every new church member. My prayer is that every follower of Christ I have the privilege of pastoring would have an intentional plan for following Jesus and fishing for men.

That's my prayer for you as well. Therefore, I invite you to walk through your own Personal Disciple-Making Plan.

Starting today and going forward, you'll encounter a straightforward question at the end of each week in this study. I've tried to keep the primary questions simple, yet I've also provided additional questions to help you flesh out what it means to follow Jesus. I don't presume that together these questions are exhaustive, but I believe they're essential. My hope and prayer are that they'll serve you as you consider what it means to follow Christ.

Without any further ado, here's the first question.

How Will You Fill Your Mind with Truth?

The life of a disciple is the life of a learner. We constantly attune our ears to the words of our Master. As He teaches us through His Word, He transforms us in the world. He changes our thoughts, our desires, our will, our relationships, and our purpose for living.

As disciples of Jesus, then, you and I must be intentional about filling our minds with His truth. In the words of Paul, "Whatever is true, whatever is honorable, whatever is just, whatever is pure, whatever is lovely, whatever is commendable, if there is any excellence, if there is anything worthy of praise, think about these things" (Phil. 4:8, ESV).

So take time to consider how you'll intentionally fill your mind with his truth. Specifically, answer the following questions.

How will you read God's Word? You might start with a plan to read a chapter a day, and maybe that plan will increase to two, three, four, or more chapters a day. You might consider using an intentional Bible-reading plan that covers all of Scripture over a certain period of time.[2] If the Bible is the revelation of God's Word to God's children, shouldn't every Christian read the whole thing?

Are you satisfied or unsatisfied with your current plan for reading God's Word? Why?

What steps can you take in the next week to advance toward a deeper study of the Bible?

How will you memorize God's Word? As you read, look for verses, paragraphs, or chapters that seem particularly significant and applicable to your life. Then commit them to memory. Again, maybe you can start by memorizing a verse a week, and then you can take on more as your hunger for hiding God's Word in your heart increases.

The apostle James commanded us to "humbly accept the word planted in you, which can save you" (Jas. 1:21). This is an important image. God's Word is like a seed that we can receive over and over in our minds and hearts—a seed that continually grows inside us and changes us from the inside out.

What obstacles are currently preventing you from memorizing God's Word?

Reflect on the benefits you'll experience as you memorize more and more of the Bible. What potential blessings do you hope to encounter through this discipline?

What practical steps will you need to take in order to realize these blessings?

How will you learn God's Word from others? Reading, studying, and understanding the Bible is not just an individual effort; it's a community project. We all need people who faithfully teach God's Word, and we all need brothers and sisters who consistently encourage us with the Scriptures. So as a member of a church and in your life as a Christian, what's your plan for consistently learning God's Word from and with others?

What obstacles currently prevent you from getting the most from your church's worship services?

How can these obstacles be overcome?

What steps can you take to interact with other Christians and discuss the Scriptures during the week?

As you consider a plan for reading, memorizing, and learning God's Word, don't forget that we do these things as disciples not for information's sake but for transformation's sake. Once again, the words of James are helpful: "Do not merely listen to the word, and so deceive yourselves. Do what it says" (Jas. 1:22).

As *believers* in Jesus, we're *followers of* Jesus, which means that we not only *hear* the truth of Christ; we *apply* the truth of Christ. Our goal as disciples is never just to believe God's Word; our goal is to obey God's Word.

THEREFORE, AS YOU PLAN TO FILL YOUR MIND WITH TRUTH,

ALSO PURPOSE TO FOLLOW THE ONE WHO IS TRUTH.

1. Elesha Coffman, "What is the origin of the Christian fish symbol?" *Christianity Today* [online], 8 August 2008 [cited 28 November 2012]. Available from the Internet: *www.christianitytoday.com*.
2. *Reader's Guide to the Bible* provides a one-year plan for reading the Bible in chronological, daily segments, along with brief commentary to help you understand your daily reading. Order item 005414497 from LifeWay Christian Resources.

DELIGHT IN GOD

Welcome back to this group discussion of *Follow Me*.

Last week's application activity involved reading the same chapter from the Bible each day and using it to examine the connection between your actions and beliefs. If you're comfortable, share what you learned during these experiences.

Describe what you liked best about the study material in week 2. What questions do you have?

What kinds of food do you crave on a regular basis?

What emotions do you experience when you give in to those cravings and eat what you desire?

To prepare to view the DVD segment, read aloud John 6:35-40:

> Jesus declared, "I am the bread of life. He who comes to me will never go hungry, and he who believes in me will never be thirsty. But as I told you, you have seen me and still you do not believe. All that the Father gives me will come to me, and whoever comes to me I will never drive away. For I have come down from heaven not to do my will but to do the will of him who sent me. And this is the will of him who sent me, that I shall lose none of all that he has given me, but raise them up at the last day. For my Father's will is that everyone who looks to the Son and believes in him shall have eternal life, and I will raise him up at the last day."

Complete the viewer guide below as you watch DVD session 3.

Belief, trust, and obedience to God's Word are the _____ of the disciple's life.

We cannot separate faith in Christ from _____ for Christ.

Christ alone can fulfill our _____.

God created us to _____.

Our cravings are designed to be satisfied by our _____.

Our deepest craving is not ultimately for something but for _____.
God has created us to be satisfied in Him.

Our satisfaction is not found ultimately in gifts but in the _____.

The trigger of sin involves looking to the things of this world to satisfy us _____
from our Creator.

The tragedy of sin is that we _____ from the One our souls long for most.

Christ alone can transform our _____.

We can conquer sin by trusting Christ to change our _____.

The power of sin to lure us away in this world is broken when our hearts are _____
with all that God is for us in Christ.

You break the power of sin by finding _____ pleasure in Christ.

This is our prayer as disciples of Jesus: "God, increase our desire for _____."

Christ alone can _____ our satisfaction.

We can live for the fleeting pleasures of this world. Or we can live for _____
pleasure in our God.

Video sessions available for purchase at *www.lifeway.com/followme*

Discuss the DVD segment with your group, using the questions below.

What did you like best from David's teaching? Why?

What are the main desires that drive the actions and attitudes of most people? What's the source of those desires?

What determines whether a desire is wholesome or sinful?

Respond to David's statement: "Our deepest craving is not ultimately for something but for Someone. God has created us to be satisfied in Him."

Do you find enjoyment and pleasure in your relationship with Jesus? Explain.

What steps can Christians take to deepen their dependence on and enjoyment of Jesus?

What do you love and long for in your everyday life that may be keeping you from experiencing a deeper love for Jesus and a greater longing for Him?

Application: Throughout this week pay special attention to any experiences you enjoy deeply. These can involve food, music, conversations, entertainment, and so on. When you encounter something that's especially enjoyable, make a conscious effort to connect that experience with God. Thank Him for blessing you and specifically praise Him as the Giver of good things and your ultimate Source of satisfaction.

Scripture: Memorize John 6:35 this week.

READ week 3 and complete the activities before the next group experience.

READ chapter 5 in the book *Follow Me* by David Platt (Tyndale, 2013).

Jesus declared, "I am the bread of life. He who comes to me will never go hungry, and he who believes in me will never be thirsty." John 6:35

Jonathan Edwards is considered by many to be America's greatest theologian. Never one to pull punches, Edwards disliked the way some churches and Christians of his day had become carried away with highly emotional worship services that were devoid of God's Word. He also disliked the way other churches and Christians claimed to hold tightly to the Word of God while their worship lacked any real emotion.

Edwards believed it was a mistake to attempt any separation between doctrinal truth and legitimate emotion. In fact, he claimed it was impossible to have one without the other:

Our external delights, our earthly pleasures, our ambition, and our reputation, our human relationships, for all these things, our desires are eager, our appetites strong, our love warm and affectionate. When it comes to these things, our hearts are tender and sensitive, deeply impressed, easily moved, much concerned and greatly engaged. ...

But when it comes to spiritual matters, how dull we feel. ... How heavy and hard our hearts; we can sit and hear of the infinite height and length and breadth and love of God and Christ Jesus, of his giving his infinitely dear Son, and yet sit there, cold and unmoved. If we are going to be excited about anything, shouldn't it be our spiritual lives? Is there anything more inspiring, more exciting, more loveable and desirable in Heaven or on Earth than the Gospel of Jesus Christ?[1]

According to Edwards, faith should fuel feeling. Intellectual knowledge of God naturally and necessarily involves emotional feeling for God. In other words, those of us who submit to God as our ultimate authority should also delight in Him as our Father.

DELIGHT IN GOD

OUR FATHER

When we returned home from Kazakhstan with Caleb, we quickly learned that people say the strangest things when they see you with a child who's clearly of another ethnicity. "He's so cute," people remark. "Do you also have children of your own?" Go ahead and write that down as phrase number one never to say to a parent who's adopted a child.

Every time we're asked this, we have an irresistible urge to say, "Come in really close because we have a secret to share. *He's ours!*"

Other times people looked at Caleb, realized that he's adopted, and then asked, "Have you met his real mother?" My response to that one is quick and clear: "Well, yes, I'm actually married to her. Her name is Heather." They respond, "Well, you know what I mean," to which I respond, "Yes, and you know what I mean. My precious wife is not his fake mother; she's *bona fide* real."

What ideas or images come to mind when you hear the word *adoption?*

You see, Caleb's our son. He's not an alien or a stranger in our family. He's not somewhat Platt, partly Platt, or kind of Platt. He's fully Platt, with all that being a Platt involves (for better or worse).

These kinds of questions and comments from well-meaning people aren't just annoyances to parents who've adopted. They're symptoms of something much deeper, for they reflect how little we understand about what it means to be adopted into a family. And if we don't understand the concept of adoption at its core, how can we realize the ramifications of what it means to become a child in the family of God?

What's your reaction to the previous statements? Why?

Clearly, when Caleb became our son, it wasn't the end of the story. It was the beginning of an adventure in which Caleb would *live* as our son. Today Caleb knows that I'm his dad and he's my son, not just because of the love I showed by traveling to Kazakhstan years ago to adopt him but because of the love I show him today. Without question, although his status in our family is based on what a judge declared years ago, his life is based on our relationship every day as we play cars, throw the baseball, run around the yard, and sing songs together.

This picture of joy in earthly adoption provides just a small glimpse of a far greater joy found in heavenly adoption. Without question our status before God was settled at the moment we turned from our sin and ourselves and trusted in Jesus as Savior and Lord. But our lives are based on the love relationship we enjoy and experience every moment of every day as God our Father saturates us as His children with His affection.

God Delights in Us

Throughout the Old Testament, God is called many magnificent names and is given a number of majestic titles, but rarely is he described as Father; that happens only 15 times, to be exact. However, when we come to the Gospels, the first four books of the New Testament, we see God described as Father 165 different times. And 164 of those descriptions occur in situations where Jesus was specifically teaching His disciples.

For example, during the Sermon on the Mount, Jesus said this while teaching His disciples how to pray: "This, then, is how you should pray: 'Our Father in heaven, hallowed be your name' " (Matt. 6:9). Amazingly, this is the first time in the Bible where anyone is encouraged to pray to God as Father.

Jesus' words are both astounding and significant. As Christians, we have the distinct privilege of knowing, worshiping, talking, and relating to God as "our Father."

Read the rest of the Lord's Prayer in Matthew 6:9-13. What do you appreciate most from these verses?

How do the words of Jesus' prayer help us relate to God as "our Father"?

This theme continues throughout the rest of the New Testament. We're told that God our Father delights in forgiving us (see Matt. 6:11-15), providing for us (see vv. 25-33), leading us (see Rom. 8:14), protecting us (see v. 15), sustaining us (see 1 Cor. 8:6), comforting us (see 2 Cor. 1:3), directing us (see 1 Thess. 3:11), purifying us (see v. 13), disciplining us (see Heb. 12:5-11), giving to us (see Jas. 1:17), calling us (see Jude 1), and promising us an inheritance (see Col. 1:12).

For which of these actions of God are you most thankful? Why?

Read three of the Scripture references listed in the previous paragraph. Then record your reaction to each reference.

1.

2.

3.

I love the culmination of this theme in 1 John 3, where you can hear the awe and excitement bursting from the apostle's words: "How great is the love the Father has lavished on us, that we should be called children of God! And that is what we are!" (v. 1).

Do you feel the weight of this? Most Christians would intellectually agree that God loves us, but have you experienced His love in an emotional way? Do you understand that God *likes* you? That He *wants* you? Have you felt God's delight in you as His child?

What's your reaction to the previous questions? Why?

We Delight in God

Don't imagine for a second that such an experience of delight was meant to be one-sided. Just as God finds great joy in loving us and caring for us as His children, we should find great joy in running to Him as Father. We should feel an overwhelming sense of love for God, and we should regularly find ways to express that love.

In other words, being a follower of Jesus involves much more than intellectual agreement with the Bible and Christian doctrine. Being a follower of Jesus involves emotional affection for Christ.

David understood this:

**One thing I ask of the Lord,
this is what I seek:
that I may dwell in the house of the Lord
all the days of my life,
to gaze upon the beauty of the Lord
and to seek him in his temple.
Psalm 27:4**

Read Psalm 30:1-12. How do these verses express David's delight in God?

Paul and Silas understood this principle, and they acted on it even after being thrown in jail and bound with chains: "About midnight Paul and Silas were praying and singing hymns to God, and the other prisoners were listening to them" (Acts 16:25).

The citizens of heaven also understand this principle:

**In a loud voice they sang:
"Worthy is the Lamb, who was slain,
to receive power and wealth and wisdom and strength
and honor and glory and praise!"
Revelation 5:12**

When have you experienced powerful moments of worshiping God?

In what other ways do you express your affection for Christ?

For a time Caleb and I did this thing where I would point at him across the room and yell, "I love Caleb!" Then he'd look back at me and yell, "I love Daddy!"

One day we were doing this, and Caleb was laughing. All of a sudden he stopped, looked at me, and said, "You love me?"

I said, "Yeah, Buddy, I do."

And then he asked what seemed to be his favorite question: "Why?"

I said, "Because you're my son."

So he asked the question again: "Why?"

This time I thought to myself, *Now that's a good question. Of all the children in the world, why is this precious little boy standing in front of me as my son?* I thought about all the factors that had come together to lead Heather and me to Kazakhstan and all the ups and downs when we wondered if we were ever going to have kids. Eventually I said: "You're our son because we wanted you. And we came to get you so that you could have a mommy and a daddy."

In this moment understand that God loves you and wants you. He *likes* you! He sacrificed more than you can imagine in order to make you His child. Don't accept His love passively. If you're a follower of Jesus, delight in following Him.

EVEN NOW RUN INTO HIS ARMS AND SAY, "MY FATHER."

JESUS SATISFIES OUR DESIRES

Desire is one characteristic that distinguishes us as human beings. We all have desires and cravings—things we want to experience, possess, or become. Sometimes our desires are the same. Everyone desires food and water, for example, especially when one or both begin to run short. Most people desire to love and be loved. Most of us also crave some form of success or accomplishment in our chosen areas of influence.

Many times our desires are different, and these differences often serve to mark us as individuals. Some people crave attention and love being in the spotlight; others prefer to remain anonymous. Some people crave exotic flavors and spices; others crave meat and potatoes.

Record three desires you've keenly felt in recent weeks.

1.

2.

3.

Do you believe your desires are primarily positive or negative? Explain.

Yesterday we introduced the concept of delighting in God and our relationship with Him as Father, just as He delights in loving us as His children. Unfortunately, our desires often become one of the obstacles that prevent us from fully experiencing such a relationship—but not in the way we typically expect.

I think many followers of Christ have become convinced their natural desires and their desire for God are mutually exclusive. In other words, they believe their craving for God is right, while all other cravings—for success, for human companionship, for excitement, for safety, and so on—are wrong. This is a false belief.

In reality, we don't have to choose between embracing our natural cravings and embracing God. Rather, God is both the source and the satisfaction of our desires.

God Is the Source

When we think about Adam and Eve in the garden of Eden, we rightly think about paradise. We think of a perfect place that was perfectly designed to meet the needs of human beings.

But we shouldn't think of Eden as a place devoid of human desire. Look at the text:

> **The LORD God had planted a garden in the east, in Eden; and there he put the man he had formed. And the LORD God made all kinds of trees grow out of the ground—trees that were pleasing to the eye and good for food. In the middle of the garden were the tree of life and the tree of the knowledge of good and evil. Genesis 2:8-9**

Just in those two verses we see the reflection of several human desires. The trees in the garden were "pleasing to the eye," which implies a human desire for beauty. They were also "good for food," which reveals a craving for physical nourishment. The "tree of life" and the "tree of the knowledge of good and evil" imply a desire for longevity and moral purpose.

So this garden paradise where Adam and Eve lived wasn't a place where humans had no needs or desires. Rather, it was a place where all of their needs and desires were met by the God who'd created them.

What's your reaction to the previous statements? Why?

Read Genesis 2:10-25. What additional human desires are reflected in these verses?

The same is true in our lives. You and I have cravings and desires; we shouldn't fight them. Indeed, we should embrace the knowledge that our cravings find their source in God. He's hardwired us with desires for water, food, friends, meaning, purpose, and much more.

We get into trouble, however, when we allow our cravings and desires to drive us away from our Creator. That's what happened with Adam and Eve:

> **"You will not surely die," the serpent said to the woman. "For God knows that when you eat of it your eyes will be opened, and you will be like God, knowing good and evil." When the woman saw that the fruit of the tree was good for food and pleasing to the eye, and also desirable for gaining wisdom, she took some and ate it. She also gave some to her husband, who was with her, and he ate it. Genesis 3:4-6**

What stands out as most interesting from these verses? Why?

What desires did Adam and Eve want to satisfy by eating the fruit?

The tragedy of this story is that Adam and Eve believed the lie that their desires could only be fulfilled apart from God—that they had to disobey God and act in secret in order to experience true pleasure. Sadly, in Adam and Eve's quest to feed their stomachs, they ended up running away from the only One who could fulfill their souls.

Even more sadly, all of us have made the same mistake.

Only God Satisfies

Many years after Adam and Eve left the garden, God worked to remind His people that He was the sole source of satisfaction for their cravings. Having been rescued from Egypt, the Israelites were wandering in the desert and desperate for food. In His mercy God sent manna—bread from heaven—and flocks of quail to feed them.

Read Exodus 16:1-12. Describe the Israelites' attitude in these verses.

What were God's motivations in providing the manna and quail?

Notice that one of God's goals in feeding His people was to satisfy their hunger—to fulfill the craving for food He'd designed them to experience. But God also intended that fulfillment to remind the Israelites that He was the sole source of satisfaction for all of their cravings. He said, "At twilight you will eat meat, and in the morning you will be filled with bread. Then you will know that I am the LORD your God" (v. 12).

After many more years Jesus used a similar teaching method while addressing large crowds of hungry people. The early verses of John 6 describe how Jesus miraculously fed five thousand men and their families, using only five barley loaves and two small fish—an event that surely reminded the people of how God had provided manna and quail to the Israelites.

The crowds found Jesus again on the following day, and they wanted more. Earlier they had eaten their fill, but now they were hungry again. Rightly, they looked to Jesus to satisfy that basic craving for food.

In what ways has God provided for your basic needs?

However, Jesus didn't want to stay on the level of basic cravings. He wanted to satisfy their deeper desires—their spiritual cravings. He said, "It was not Moses who gave you the bread from heaven, but my Father gives you the true bread from heaven" (John 6:32, ESV). Jesus made it clear that the bread that comes from God is far superior to the manna that came through Moses. Naturally, the crowds demanded, "Give us this bread" (v. 34), and in that way the stage was set for a startling declaration.

"I am the bread of life," Jesus declared. "He who comes to me will never go hungry, and he who believes in me will never be thirsty" (v. 35). In one sweeping statement Jesus communicated to the crowds that He Himself was the provision of God sent to satisfy their souls. Jesus said to the crowds, in effect, "If you want to be fulfilled, put your faith in Me."

How have you experienced Jesus as the "bread of life"?

Jesus' declarations have huge implications for those who want to understand what it means to follow Him. To come to Jesus, or to believe in Jesus, is to look to Him to satisfy your soul forever. To come to Jesus is to taste and see that He is good (see Ps. 34:8) and to find in Him the end of all your desires.

JESUS IS BOTH THE SOURCE AND THE SATISFACTION

OF OUR DESIRES, AND TO FOLLOW HIM IS TO EXPERIENCE

AN ETERNAL PLEASURE THAT FAR OUTWEIGHS AND

OUTLASTS THE TEMPORAL PLEASURES OF THIS WORLD.

JESUS OFFERS TRUE PLEASURE

Most Christians can get behind the idea that Jesus is our Provider, which means He satisfies our desire for food, water, shelter, and so on. We also know Jesus is our Lord, which means He fulfills our craving for meaning and purpose in life. And ultimately, we understand that Jesus is our Savior, which means He satisfies our desire for forgiveness and eternal life.

But what about pleasure? What about our daily desire to feel not just fulfilled but also happy? What about our need to seize the day and regularly squeeze some joy out of life?

After all, it's one thing to deal with a craving for food by eating a bowl of white rice. That will satisfy your hunger. But as someone who's lived in New Orleans, I can tell you it's a totally different experience to deal with that craving by eating a plate of seafood gumbo with hush puppies and a beignet for dessert. That will give you pleasure.

What ideas or images come to mind when you hear the word *pleasure?*

Do you believe seeking opportunities to experience pleasure is a positive or negative goal? Explain.

Seeking Pleasure

As followers of Jesus, we believe that He's the only way for us to find forgiveness from sin and experience eternal life. That's clear from God's Word: "Jesus answered, 'I am the way and the truth and the life. No one comes to the Father except through me' " (John 14:6).

Yet many Christians also believe the world has cornered the market when it comes to providing pleasure. Whether or not we'd say it out loud, we feel that we need to step away from following Jesus when we can no longer resist the urge to have a little fun.

What activities have you sought as a way to have fun and experience pleasure in recent months?

How are those activities connected with your commitment to follow Christ?

Because of this way of thinking, many Christians view salvation as a business transaction—an agreement that involves letting go of the things in the world we love in order to accept things that, if we're really honest, we loathe. We may be willing to "make a decision for Christ" in order to save our skin for eternity, but if the truth were told, we really like the ways of this world, and we really want the things of this world because of the pleasure they bring.

So we're caught in the middle. We know we're supposed to try hard to follow Christ. Yet deep down the pleasures, pursuits, plaudits, and possessions of this world seem far more enticing. This is why the lives of Christians are often indistinguishable from the lives of non-Christians. We profess to have faith in Christ, yet we're just as sensualistic, just as humanistic, and just as materialistic as the world around us.

What's your reaction to the previous statements?

When have you felt caught between your desire to follow Jesus and your desire to experience pleasure? What happened next?

What's the answer, then? Do we become better Christians by working harder to beat down our desire for pleasure? Do we resign ourselves to lives of sterile routine and cold contentment?

No. The solution isn't to abandon our search for pleasure—it's to search for more pleasure. We must seek the kind of happiness and joy that come from truly delighting in Christ and allowing Him to change our affections.

Seeking Pleasure Through Christ

I love what C. S. Lewis wrote about this topic:

> **If we consider the unblushing promises of reward and the staggering nature of the rewards promised in the Gospels, it would seem that our Lord finds our desires not too strong, but too weak. We are half-hearted creatures, fooling about with drink and sex and ambition when infinite joy is offered us, like an ignorant child who wants to go on making mud pies in a slum because he cannot imagine what is meant by the offer of a holiday at the sea. We are far too easily pleased.**[2]

John 6 records Jesus speaking to several of those "half-hearted creatures"—people who were more interested in a mouthful of bread than a life-changing encounter with the Creator of the universe. A couple of chapters earlier, Jesus had a similar conversation with a half-hearted woman drawing water from a well.

Read John 4:4-15. What strikes you as most interesting from these verses?

How do Jesus' words in John 4 compare with His declarations about the "bread of life" in John 6?

What's interesting about the end of Jesus' conversation with the Samaritan woman is that He made an effort to expose her sin. He told her straight out that she'd had five husbands and was currently living with a man who wasn't her husband (v. 18). In other words, she was an adulterer.

Why did Jesus expose the woman that way? Because He wanted her to have a clear picture of the trajectory of her life. She'd been trying to satisfy her desires in ways that were outside of God's will. She'd adopted the world's methods for finding pleasure, and they weren't working. Her life was a mess.

Jesus offered her a better alternative: Himself. After the woman unsuccessfully tried to change the subject by talking about the coming Messiah, Jesus dropped a bombshell: "Jesus declared, 'I who speak to you am he' " (v. 26).

Read John 4:27-42. What were the results of the woman's encounter with Jesus?

When did you first encounter Jesus as Messiah?

When Jesus transforms our desires, we realize the problems we have with sin in this world are not because we want pleasure too much; it's because we want pleasure too little. It's tragic when so many so-called Christians endlessly chase the next temptation, the bigger house, the nicer possession, the newer pursuit, the greater notoriety, the higher success, and the more comfortable lifestyle. Such a quest for pleasure in this world reflects a lack of contentment in Christ. Moreover, it reflects a lack of connection with Christ.

True disciples of Jesus have learned to gladly forsake the trinkets this world offers—sex, money, pride, success, and so on—because they've found surpassing treasure in Christ. They've found pleasure in Christ.

What's your reaction to the previous statements? Why?

In what ways do you experience pleasure through your relationship with Jesus?

I'm not saying every opportunity for pleasure in the world is wrong or should be avoided. God has given us many gifts that we should enjoy—gifts that should bring us pleasure. Our taste buds are formed to find pleasure in good food. Our eyes are made to find pleasure in magnificent scenery. Our ears are fashioned to find pleasure in beautiful music. Our bodies are designed to find pleasure in physical intimacy with a spouse.

But amid all these pleasures we're wired to pursue, we must always remember that our deepest craving is not for something but for Someone. Our ultimate satisfaction is found not in the gifts we enjoy but in the Giver who provides them:

THE BREAD OF GOD IS HE WHO COMES DOWN FROM HEAVEN AND GIVES LIFE TO THE WORLD. JOHN 6:33

EXAMINING THE CHRISTIAN LIFE

Over the course of my life, I've met very few people who enjoy doing chores around the house—things like taking out the trash, cleaning the bathroom, washing dishes, and so on.

Most of the time we approach such tasks with a simple lack of motivation. We don't really want to do them, but we know they're necessary. So we buckle down. Other times, however, we actively dislike performing specific chores. We hate them and must be forced or nagged before we'll carry them out.

What chores do you most dislike in your household? Record three.

1.

2.

3.

I'm afraid many followers of Jesus have incorporated a number of religious chores into their daily Christian lives. They believe there are certain tasks every Christian must perform even if they lack the motivation—even if they honestly dislike performing them.

Worse, I'm afraid many so-called Christians use these religious chores as a way to verify their Christian identity and justify their worldly practices. For example, many would-be followers of Christ attempt to excuse their inappropriate behavior on Friday night because they go to church on Sunday morning. They believe viewing pornography or engaging in gossip isn't as big a deal if they had a quiet time earlier in the day. Such ideas reflect the influence of superficial religion, which we explored earlier in this study.

What's your reaction to the previous statements? Why?

So today I want to step back and examine our motivations for living the Christian life. Why as Christians do we do the things we do? And what do our motivations communicate about our relationship with Christ?

Why Do Christians Read the Bible?

To people who haven't been born again, the words of Scripture seem tedious, dull, or even ridiculous. But to those who are followers of Jesus—to men and women whose hearts have been transformed by the passionate pursuit and faithful love of Christ—His words are priceless. They aren't merely read; they're reflected on. They're not merely examined; they're enjoyed. They're not merely analyzed; they're applied.

This is how people in the Bible talk about God's Word. Listen to this psalm, for example:

> **Oh, how I love your law!**
> **I meditate on it all day long.**
> **Your commands make me wiser than my enemies,**
> **for they are ever with me.**
> **I have more insight than all my teachers,**
> **for I meditate on your statutes.**
> **Psalm 119:97-99**

Read the following passages of Scripture and record what they communicate about God's Word.

Psalm 19:7-11

Psalm 119:169-176

What emotions do you experience when you read God's Word? Why?

When Jesus had completed his fast of 40 days in the wilderness, Scripture says, "He was hungry" (Matt. 4:2). Well, of course! Scripture also says Satan came to tempt Him in that moment of physical weakness, suggesting that Jesus transform stones into bread and create something to eat. Jesus replied by quoting a verse from Deuteronomy:

> **Jesus answered, "It is written: 'Man does not live on bread alone, but on every word that comes from the mouth of God.' " Matthew 4:4**

Those weren't just empty words on the part of our Savior. For true disciples of Christ, the Bible is our daily bread. It's more important, more valuable, more treasured, and more desired than even breakfast, lunch, and dinner. In other words, disciples of Jesus read the Bible because they *want* to read it, not because they're supposed to.

So what about you? Do you love God's Word? When you open it, is it like you've discovered valuable treasure? Are the words on the page the joy of your heart?

What's your reaction to the previous questions?

How can you work with the Holy Spirit to increase your affection for God's Word?

Why Do Christians Pray?

In a similar way, true disciples of Jesus pray because they crave communication with God. They deeply desire to feel connected with Christ and involve Him in every decision they face; therefore, they find ways to "pray continually" (1 Thess. 5:17).

Yet we are prone to miss this. Most of us have learned to pray and think about prayer as simply asking for things. "Bless me, help me, protect me, and provide for me"—these are often the only words from our mouths when we bow our heads. Our prayers are filled with a list of the things we need and the stuff we want. Consequently, in prayer we're pleased when God responds in the way we've asked, and we're perplexed when He doesn't.

Do these descriptions match your practice of prayer? Explain.

But what if prayer isn't primarily about giving God a to-do list? After all, Jesus told His disciples that their "Father knows what [they] need before [they] ask him" (Matt. 6:8).

The purpose of prayer isn't for a disciple to bring information to God; the purpose of prayer is for the disciple to experience intimacy with God. That's why Jesus said to His disciples, "When you pray, go into your room, close the door and pray to your Father, who is unseen" (Matt. 6:6). Find a place, Jesus said. Set aside a time. Get alone with God.

I believe this one practice will utterly revolutionize your life, not just your prayer life but your entire life. Something happens that can't be described in words when a disciple is alone with God. In a quiet place, behind closed doors, when you or I commune with the infinitely great, indescribably good God of the universe, we experience a joy to which no person or no thing in this world can even begin to compare.

Are you satisfied with your current prayer life? Why or why not?

What are the primary motivations that drive you to pray?

Why Do Christians Worship?

Why do we worship God? Because we *want* God. We exalt Him precisely because we enjoy Him. Think of the way sports fans continually sing the praises of their favorite athletes. Think of the way newlyweds regularly lift up and exalt their spouses. Think of the way people crow about their favorite meals, songs, movies, or books.

Isn't that the essence of worship? When you delight in something, you can't help but declare that delight. When you adore someone, you automatically announce your adoration; you can't wait to tell people about it!

Therefore, true followers of Christ gladly use our lips and our lives to lift up the One we love above all others. We delight in worshiping God.

In what worship activities do you regularly participate?

Do you enjoy those activities? Explain.

The central question, then, is clear: Are you delighting in God? Are you emotionally overwhelmed, even at this moment, by the thought that you're His child? Have you truly tasted His transcendent pleasure in a way that provokes you to read His Word, pray, worship, fast, give, and share the gospel—in addition to hosts of other actions compelled by your affection for God?

THIS IS THE **HEART** OF FOLLOWING JESUS:

ENJOYING GOD AS FATHER THROUGH CHRIST THE SON.

PERSONAL DISCIPLE-MAKING PLAN: HOW TO FUEL YOUR AFFECTION FOR GOD

Today marks the halfway point in this study, and you may feel a little beaten up right now. You may feel convicted. You may feel attacked. You may wish you had a stronger relationship with Christ or a deeper desire for Him. You may even wonder whether you're actually a Christian.

If you're experiencing those kinds of reactions, I understand. I've experienced all of them and more during the process of writing this study. And that's good. We're discussing challenging principles and answering difficult questions, so we should feel the weight of those encounters.

But let me also encourage you not to remain under that weight so long that it crushes you. Don't waste time chastising yourself. Don't allow yourself to become so discouraged that you default to the status quo or give up on the idea of serving Christ altogether.

Instead, commit to move forward. And commit to doing so with God's help. If you've identified areas you can improve as a follower of Jesus, pledge to do all you can to improve, starting with this Personal Disciple-Making Plan. Then ask God for the strength and conviction to achieve anything else that's needed.

Trust me: you can move forward as a follower of Jesus who delights in God and makes an impact on the world around you.

How Will You Worship?

The Bible reminds us that all of life is worship. Every experience is an opportunity to declare our delight in God and praise His name.

To the church in Rome, Paul wrote, "I urge you, brothers, in view of God's mercy, to offer your bodies as living sacrifices, holy and pleasing to God—this is your spiritual act of worship" (Rom. 12:1). To the church in Corinth, Paul said, "Whether you eat or drink or whatever you do, do it all for the glory of God" (1 Cor. 10:31). These instructions apply to us as well.

Aside from church services, when do you typically make an effort to worship God?

Are you typically satisfied with the results of your worship? Explain.

What steps can you take to focus on worshiping God during the everyday routines of your life?

In addition to your individual worship, remember Scripture's clear exhortation to meet regularly with the church for worship (see Heb. 10:24-25). Commit to gathering weekly with brothers and sisters to collectively express your desire for and delight in God.

What steps can you take to make the most of your experiences at church?

How Will You Pray?

Jesus said, "When you pray, go into your room, close the door and pray to your Father, who is unseen" (Matt. 6:6). In other words, find yourself a place and set aside a time to be with the Father. Yes, God's Word teaches us to "pray continually" (1 Thess. 5:17), but I've found that concentrated prayer at a specific point in time is the best fuel for continual prayer all the time.

What time and place will you set aside for communion with your Father this week?

What barriers will you need to remove in order to consistently practice this discipline of prayer?

This kind of focused, concentrated prayer comes with a reward. That's the second part of Matthew 6:6: "When you pray, go into your room, close the door and pray to your Father, who is unseen. *Then your Father, who sees what is done in secret, will reward you*" (emphasis added).

This reward is deeply emotional. Through prayer we experience awe-inspiring adoration and affection for God. We experience heartbreaking confession and contrition because of our sin. And we experience breathtaking gratitude and praise because our sins are forgiven. In addition, we're given the opportunity to cry out for God to meet our deepest needs. We share the desires of our souls, not because we want to give God information but because we trust in His provision.

Prayer affords us moments of deep, personal connection with God—moments that bring us both satisfaction and pleasure.

Describe what you enjoy most about your experiences in prayer.

What are your long-term goals for achieving a deeper connection with God in prayer?

What steps can you take in the short term to move toward those goals?

How Will You Fast?

The idea of fasting may be altogether new to you, but Jesus' words to His disciples seem to imply that they should regularly set aside food in order to feast on God alone:

> **When you fast, do not look somber as the hypocrites do, for they disfigure their faces to show men they are fasting. I tell you the truth, they have received their reward in full. But when you fast, put oil on your head and wash your face, so that it will not be obvious to men that you are fasting, but only to your Father, who is unseen; and your Father, who sees what is done in secret, will reward you. Matthew 6:16-18**

Have your past experiences with fasting been positive or negative? Why?

What do you hope to achieve through the practice of fasting?

If you've never fasted before, I encourage you to start by setting aside one meal each week. When the times comes for that breakfast, lunch, or dinner, take the hour you would have spent eating and instead spend it praying or reading God's Word.

Once you've grown accustomed to this practice and discovered the value of this time—an hour alone with God will quickly prove quite fulfilling, trust me—plan to fast for two meals in one day, and then for an entire 24-hour period. As you grow in fasting, you may consider fasting for consecutive days on a periodic basis. Regardless, plan to fast from food so that you can learn to feast on God and delight in Him.

What meal will you skip this week in order to feast on God and His Word?

What steps can you take to create a regular schedule for the discipline of fasting?

How Will You Give?

When you think about fueling your affection for God, giving may not be the first thing that comes to mind. But Jesus' teaching on giving in Scripture was directly associated with His teaching on fasting and praying. Indeed, immediately after He taught His disciples about praying and fasting, He said these words:

> **Do not store up for yourselves treasures on earth, where moth and rust destroy, and where thieves break in and steal. But store up for yourselves treasures in heaven, where moth and rust do not destroy, and where thieves do not break in and steal. For where your treasure is, there your heart will be also. Matthew 6:19-21**

Notice the tie between our money and our affections. According to Jesus, our money doesn't just reflect our hearts; our hearts actually follow our money. Therefore, one of the most effective ways to fuel affection for God is to give your resources in obedience to Him.

What are your current habits when it comes to giving money, possessions, and time for God's kingdom?

What have been the primary motivations for your giving?

As a disciple of Jesus, how will you intentionally, generously, sacrificially, and cheerfully give to the church and to those in need around you?

How will you give to those in need around the world?

Following Jesus involves not only intellectual trust in Him but also emotional desire for Him. We've seen that it's impossible to separate true faith in Christ from profound feelings for Christ.

THEREFORE, AS DISCIPLES OF JESUS, WE INTENTIONALLY

WORSHIP, PRAY, FAST, AND GIVE IN ORDER

TO FUEL OUR AFFECTION FOR GOD.

1. Jonathan Edwards, *Religious Affections,* abridged and updated by Ellyn Sanna (Uhrichsville, OH: Barbour Publishing, 1999), 46–48.
2. C. S. Lewis, "The Weight of Glory," in *The Weight of Glory: And Other Addresses* (New York: HarperCollins, 2001), 26.

GOD'S WILL FOR YOUR LIFE

Welcome back to this group discussion of *Follow Me*.

Last week's application activity involved recognizing God as the ultimate Source of your most enjoyable experiences. Describe one or two of your favorite experiences from the past week.

How were those experiences affected when you intentionally connected them with God?

Describe what you liked best about the study material in week 3. What questions do you have?

How would you describe God's will for your life? Explain.

To prepare to view the DVD segment, read aloud Acts 1:4-9:

> On one occasion, while he was eating with them, he gave them this command: "Do not leave Jerusalem, but wait for the gift my Father promised, which you have heard me speak about. For John baptized with water, but in a few days you will be baptized with the Holy Spirit." So when they met together, they asked him, "Lord, are you at this time going to restore the kingdom to Israel?" He said to them: "It is not for you to know the times or dates the Father has set by his own authority. But you will receive power when the Holy Spirit comes on you; and you will be my witnesses in Jerusalem, and in all Judea and Samaria, and to the ends of the earth." After he said this, he was taken up before their very eyes, and a cloud hid him from their sight.

Discuss the DVD segment with your group, using the questions below.

What did you like best from David's teaching? Why?

What methods have you used to try and identify God's will for your life? What happened next?

Respond to David's statement: "Far more important than asking, 'What is God's will for my life?' I want to ask, 'Will you obey God's will for your life, no matter what it is?' "

As a group, review the 10 reasons David listed why we should give God a blank check with our lives. Which reasons are most compelling to you? Why?

In your own words, summarize God's will for the world. How does this impact His will for individual Christians?

What role does the Holy Spirit play in the lives of Christians?

How have you personally encountered the Holy Spirit in recent months?

Application: Throughout this week carry a blank piece of paper wherever you go as a reminder of David's challenge to offer God a blank check with your life. Offer a prayer of submission to God whenever you encounter this paper, affirming your desire to obey His will for your life, no matter what His will may be.

Scripture: Memorize Acts 1:8 this week.

READ week 4 and complete the activities before the next group experience.

READ chapter 6 in the book *Follow Me* by David Platt (Tyndale, 2013).

This Week's Scripture Memory

You will receive power when the Holy Spirit comes on you; and you will be my witnesses in Jerusalem, and in all Judea and Samaria, and to the ends of the earth. Acts 1:8

A member of our church named Matthew served for many years alongside Christians in a severely persecuted area of the world. Coming to Christ in this almost exclusively Muslim nation was extremely costly.

Matthew told me when those people come to faith in Christ, they're asked to make a list of all the unbelievers they know—typically almost everyone they know. Next the new believers are asked to circle the names of the 10 people who are least likely to kill them for becoming a Christian. Then they share the gospel as quickly as possible with each person whose name has been circled. That's why the gospel is spreading in that country.

That process sounds a lot like Matthew 4, doesn't it? " 'Follow me,' Jesus said, 'and I will make you fishers of men' " (Matt. 4:19). As soon as people become followers of Jesus, they begin fishing for men.

Sadly, this isn't the case for many—maybe most—of the professing Christians in the world. Many have hardly ever shared the gospel of Jesus Christ with even one other person at any point in their Christian lives. Even among those who've shared the gospel, most aren't actively, regularly leading people around them to follow Jesus.

Why is that? Why are so few followers of Christ personally fishing for men when this priority is designed to be central in every Christian's life? Could it be because we've fundamentally misunderstood the central purpose for which God created us? And could it be that, as a result, we're completely missing one of the chief pleasures God has planned for us?

As Jesus transforms our thoughts and desires, He revolutionizes our very reason for living. Understanding this truth is essential for knowing and experiencing the will of God as a disciple of Jesus.

GOD'S WILL FOR YOUR LIFE

KNOW GOD

Like everybody else in the world, followers of Jesus are confronted every day with a number of decisions we have to make. Each of these decisions typically carries a number of options, and each option is typically connected to a number of questions.

Often these questions aren't very significant. Where should I eat today? What should I wear today? How should I respond to this e-mail? When should I call that person? How long should I stay here? Do I want fries with that?

At other times these questions involve large, life-altering decisions. Should I date? If so, whom should I date? Should I go to college? What career path should I choose? Should I marry? If so, whom should I marry? Should we have kids? Where should I live?

Do you find it easy or difficult to make decisions? Why?

What emotions do you experience when you have to make important or difficult decisions?

All people find themselves buried under this onslaught of questions, options, and decisions. But those of us who claim to be Christians have a different perspective on that experience, because all of our little questions point back to one big question: What is God's will for my life?

Of course, that question leads us to another big question: How do I find God's will for my life?

What steps have you taken in the past to determine God's will for your life?

What was the result of those steps?

I wonder, however, if these are the questions we should be asking. Indeed, I wonder whether our preoccupation with seeking God's will for our lives has actually kept us from finding the satisfaction and purpose we all desire as followers of Christ.

God's Ultimate Concern

After *Radical* was published, I started receiving all kinds of questions and comments about specific facets of the Christian life in America. People asked me: What does a radical lifestyle look like? What kind of car should I drive? What kind of house should I live in? Am I supposed to adopt? Am I supposed to move overseas to an international mission field?

I found these questions, though sincere and honest, to be a bit troubling. It felt that people were looking for a box to check or a criterion to follow that would ensure they were obeying God— a common temptation that has its roots in superficial religion.

Please hear me: simply knowing and trusting God is far more important than searching for God's will. We yearn for mechanical formulas and easy answers because we want to find shortcuts to the mind of God. But this isn't God's design—or, I should say, this isn't God's will.

God's ultimate concern isn't to get you or me from point A to point B along the quickest, easiest, smoothest, clearest route possible. Rather, His ultimate concern is that you and I would know Him more deeply as we trust Him more completely.

Throughout your Christian walk, what has helped you most when it comes to knowing God more deeply?

What has helped you most when it comes to trusting God more completely?

Remember that becoming a disciple of Jesus means He transforms not only our minds and emotions but also our wills. Having come to Christ, we've died to ourselves and can say along with the apostle Paul, "I have been crucified with Christ and I no longer live, but Christ lives in me" (Gal. 2:20).

As Paul taught the believers in Rome, this dying to ourselves is precisely what we illustrate through baptism when we first become Christians:

> **Don't you know that all of us who were baptized into Christ Jesus were baptized into his death? We were therefore buried with him through baptism into death in order that, just as Christ was raised from the dead through the glory of the Father, we too may live a new life. Romans 6:3-4**

What ideas or images come to mind when you hear the word *baptism?*

What emotions did you experience when you were baptized? Why?

Our Blank Check

At the church I have the privilege of serving as the pastor, we talk a lot about giving God a blank check with our lives. That's because, as followers of Christ, we've surrendered the right to determine the direction of our lives. We don't choose where we live or how we live; we don't choose whether we marry or whom we marry; we don't choose what we keep or what we give away.

Jesus determines all of these things. He is our Lord and Master. As Paul wrote:

> **Do you not know that your body is a temple of the Holy Spirit, who is in you, whom you have received from God? You are not your own; you were bought at a price. 1 Corinthians 6:19-20**

In what ways have you allowed Jesus to take control of your life as Master?

Read the following passages of Scripture and record what they teach about Jesus' place as the Lord of our lives.

Matthew 6:24

2 Corinthians 4:4-5

Philippians 2:5-11

Are you willing to surrender total control over your life to Jesus? Are you willing to give Him that blank check? I can tell you that doing so won't be easy or without sacrifice. Jesus will ask much of you, just as He asked much of His first disciples.

After all, it was Jesus who said, "If anyone would come after me, he must deny himself and take up his cross daily and follow me" (Luke 9:23). It was also Jesus who said, "Go! I am sending you out like lambs among wolves" (10:3). And it was Jesus who said, "If anyone comes to me and does not hate his father and mother, his wife and children, his brothers and sisters—yes, even his own life—he cannot be my disciple" (14:26).

What's your reaction to the previous verses?

What do you fear most about offering Jesus a blank check with your life?

Giving our lives to Jesus is never easy, but it's always worth it. God is worthy of our surrender. He is worthy of our total submission and complete obedience. And remember: He loves us as our Father.

So let me encourage you to stop seeking out God's will for your life. Instead of asking that big question, I challenge you to make this bold statement: "Lord, I'll obey Your will for my life. Whatever You ask me to do, I'll do."

ARE YOU READY?

Determine what statement you're willing to make for God and record it below.

MAKING DISCIPLES

Sometimes in life a statement will catch you off guard and demand your attention. You'll hear a proclamation or statistic and think, *What? How in the world could that be true?*

I recently had that kind of experience as I was reading through the Book of Acts. It was the first two verses that got me:

In my former book, Theophilus, I wrote about all that Jesus began to do and to teach until the day he was taken up to heaven, after giving instructions through the Holy Spirit to the apostles he had chosen. Acts 1:1-2

What strikes you as most interesting in these verses? Why?

The "former book" Luke mentioned was the Gospel of Luke, of course, which is crazy when we focus on that word *began*. Began? Think of everything described in the Gospel of Luke: Jesus' birth in Bethlehem, His baptism at the hands of John the Baptist, His temptation in the wilderness, the calling of the disciples, the healing of diseases, the restoration of sight and speech, the transfiguration, Jesus' parables and sermons, His clashes with the Pharisees, His crucifixion, His resurrection, and more.

According to Luke, all of that was merely the *beginning* of what Jesus planned to do and teach! If I were reading the Book of Acts for the first time, I would be very anxious to see what Jesus accomplished as He continued His ministry.

But there's a problem. We see it in verse 2 when Luke referenced "the day [Jesus] was taken up to heaven." We see it more fully in verses 9-11:

After he said this, he was taken up before their very eyes, and a cloud hid him from their sight. They were looking intently up into the sky as he was going, when suddenly two men dressed in white stood beside them. "Men of Galilee," they said, "why do you stand here looking into the sky? This same Jesus, who has been taken from you into heaven, will come back in the same way you have seen him go into heaven."

How do these verses affect your interpretation of Acts 1:1-2?

If Jesus ascended to heaven, how could He continue what He began to do and teach during His public ministry? We'll explore that question today. We'll also explore how Jesus' work in the world intersects with our desire to find God's will for our lives.

Jesus Is Working

As we read the Book of Acts, we see several instances where Jesus directly appeared to individuals or intervened in specific circumstances to accomplish His mission in the world. His confrontation of Saul is a good example:

> **As he neared Damascus on his journey, suddenly a light from heaven flashed around him. He fell to the ground and heard a voice say to him, "Saul, Saul, why do you persecute me?" "Who are you, Lord?" Saul asked. "I am Jesus, whom you are persecuting," he replied. "Now get up and go into the city, and you will be told what you must do." Acts 9:3-6**

How did Saul's conversion contribute to the advancement of God's kingdom on earth?

Read Acts 9:10-19. What were the short-term and long-term consequences of Jesus' conversation with Ananias?

In Acts 10 Jesus spoke to Peter through a vision while the apostle was praying on a rooftop. Through that vision He showed Peter that all things created by God can be made pure by God—a revelation that paved the way for Peter's eventual ministry to the Gentiles.

Read Acts 10:9-22. What words or images strike you as most interesting in these verses? Why?

When has God convicted you to change your way of life or abandon specific behaviors? What happened next?

Jesus is fully capable of advancing His kingdom in the world without being physically present in the world. But there are also many examples in the Book of Acts of Jesus working through people who'd surrendered to His will.

Read the following passages of Scripture and record what Jesus accomplished through the actions of human beings.

Acts 1:21-26

Acts 9:32-35

Acts 16:13-15

Page after page in the Book of Acts we see Jesus working to advance His kingdom. Sometimes He chose to labor on His own, other times He chose to work through the actions of His people. But the central idea we need to understand is that Jesus was working to advance His kingdom in the world.

Moreover, we need to understand that Jesus is *still* working to advance His kingdom. He hasn't stopped. He's working to accomplish His purposes in your community, in your city, in your country, and among all nations of the earth.

The question we need to answer, then, is this: Will we join Him? Will we surrender to His will so that He can use us in the same way He used the first disciples?

What's your response to the previous questions?

God's Will for Us

Yesterday I made the statement that committing to know God and obey His commands is far more important than seeking to identify His will for our lives. One reason this is true is that following Christ means surrendering our will in submission to His will. It means our lives are literally subsumed in His life.

In other words, there's no point in trying to find God's will for our individual lives after we follow Jesus because our individual lives no longer exist. We've been crucified with Christ and now have Christ living in us (see Gal. 2:20). We're members of the body of Christ (see 1 Cor. 12:27).

We don't need to find God's will for us as individuals in the world. Rather, we need to submit to God's will for the world.

What's your reaction to the previous statements?

Fortunately, Jesus clearly identified His will for the world—and for those who would follow Him— before ascending into heaven:

> **He said to them: "It is not for you to know the times or dates the Father has set by his own authority. But you will receive power when the Holy Spirit comes on you; and you will be my witnesses in Jerusalem, and in all Judea and Samaria, and to the ends of the earth." Acts 1:7-8**

What do these verses communicate about God's will for the world?

As followers of Jesus, how do we participate in God's will for the world?

Read Matthew 28:19-20. How do these verses compare with Acts 1:7-8?

God's will for the world is to redeem men and women from every nation, tribe, language, and people. His will is to accomplish this redemption by His grace and for His glory.

Therefore, God's will for us as followers of Jesus is that we make disciples. That's our purpose. That's how we participate in Jesus' work of advancing His kingdom in this world.

What emotions do you experience when you think about God's will for His followers? Why?

How has your life been impacted by God's desire to redeem men and women from every nation, tribe, language, and people?

The more we understand God's will for the world and walk in submission to Him, the more we'll understand how foolish it is to think He would ever want to hide His will from us. Instead, we'll realize that God's desire for us to know His will is exponentially greater than our desire to know it.

As we'll explore tomorrow, God wants us to know His will so much that He's revealed it to us over and over through His Word.

AND AS WE'LL EXPLORE LATER THIS WEEK,

HE WANTS US TO EXPERIENCE HIS WILL

SO MUCH THAT HE'S GIVEN US HIS SPIRIT.

OUR GUARANTEE

If you've recently purchased an appliance or electronic device, you've probably been offered or asked to purchase some form of guarantee. These programs are called by a variety of names—extended warranty, product-replacement plan, money-back guarantee, and so on—but the basic idea is the same: if something unexpectedly goes wrong with the product, you're covered.

Whether such guarantees are worth anything depends on the company through which they're offered. Claims of "Satisfaction guaranteed!" ring hollow when they come from discount chains or questionable vendors on the Internet. But a guarantee from a reputable company can go a long way toward helping customers feel that they're making a wise purchase—a prudent investment of their resources.

What ideas or images come to mind when you hear the word *guarantee?*

How do you evaluate whether a guarantee is trustworthy?

As we saw yesterday, God's will is to redeem men and women from every nation, tribe, language, and people by His grace and for His glory. That's what He's working to achieve in the world, and He's invited us to participate. He's invited us to follow Him in that mission by surrendering our own wills in order to make disciples.

The fact that we've been offered such a privilege is wonderful news, but there's more. We've also been given a guarantee through the Word of God that our efforts and sacrifices to invest in God's work will not be in vain. We can feel free to give our lives and go wherever God leads us because we know the Bible has guaranteed what will come to pass.

Let's explore that guarantee today. When we're finished, you'll see that God's will to redeem men and women from every people group isn't limited to the Book of Acts. Rather, it's written from cover to cover throughout the Scriptures.

God's Will in the Old Testament

At the beginning of history, recorded in the Book of Genesis, God created Adam and Eve to enjoy His grace and live in a perfect relationship with Him. But God never intended for that relationship to be static. Indeed, in a very straightforward way, Adam and Eve were commissioned to be fruitful and fill the earth with followers of God:

> **God created man in his own image, in the image of God he created him; male and female he created them. God blessed them and said to them, "Be fruitful and increase in number; fill the earth and subdue it. Rule over the fish of the sea and the birds of the air and over every living creature that moves on the ground." Genesis 1:27-28**

How did God intend for Adam and Eve to participate in His will for the world?

Sadly, we know things went wrong in the Garden of Eden. Adam and Eve sinned, and their sin created a separation between human beings and God.

Still, God didn't abandon humanity. Even as our most distant ancestors spread the infection of sin around the globe, God chose to create a people for Himself—to repair the relationship that had been severed by Adam and Eve. He blessed Abraham and the other patriarchs, intending for that blessing to spread to all people.

Read the following passages of Scripture and record how they reflect God's will to redeem men and women from every tribe and nation.

Genesis 12:1-3

Genesis 26:1-6

Genesis 28:10-15

God's will for the world is reflected not only in the narrative passages of Scripture but also in the praises of His people:

> **May God be gracious to us and bless us**
> **and make his face shine upon us,**
> **that your ways may be known on earth,**
> **your salvation among all nations.**
>
> **May the peoples praise you, O God;**
> **may all the peoples praise you.**
> **May the nations be glad and sing for joy,**
> **for you rule the peoples justly**
> **and guide the nations of the earth.**
> **Psalm 67:1-4**

How can we express compassion and hope for the people in our spheres of influence who aren't following Jesus?

How can we express compassion and concern for people groups around the world that have limited access to God's Word?

The prophets also echoed the psalmist's cry. Even as they strove to warn the Israelites about idolatry and their failure to carry out God's will, the prophets regularly reminded their listeners about God's desire to save all peoples and make disciples of all nations.

Read the following passages of Scripture and record what they communicate about God's will.

Isaiah 66:18-19

Habakkuk 2:14

God's Will in the New Testament

God's will to be worshiped among the nations is also expressed throughout the New Testament. We've already seen, for example, that Jesus ended His time on earth by commanding His followers to go to the nations. He told His disciples to make disciples, preach the gospel, and proclaim His glory to the ends of the earth (see Matt. 28:19-20).

But when we look a few chapters earlier in the Book of Matthew, we find an amazing promise in the words of Jesus:

> **Because of the increase of wickedness, the love of most will grow cold, but he who stands firm to the end will be saved. And this gospel of the kingdom will be preached in the whole world as a testimony to all nations, and then the end will come. Matthew 24:12-14**

What promise did Jesus give in these verses?

What warning did Jesus give in these verses?

Jesus said His gospel *"will* be preached in the whole world" (v. 14, emphasis added). In Acts 1 He said His disciples *"will* be [His] witnesses in Jerusalem, and in all Judea and Samaria, and to the ends of the earth" (v. 8, emphasis added). These are affirmative statements from the mouth of Jesus that leave no room for doubt. They're our guarantee.

In addition, the Book of Revelation gives us a picture of what things will look like when Jesus' words come to pass:

> **After this I looked and there before me was a great multitude that no one could count, from every nation, tribe, people and language, standing before the throne and in front of the Lamb. They were wearing white robes and were holding palm branches in their hands. And they cried out in a loud voice: "Salvation belongs to our God, who sits on the throne, and to the Lamb." Revelation 7:9-10**

What strikes you as most interesting in these verses? Why?

How do these verses impact the mission and purpose of your life?

This is God's will in the world: to create, call, save, and bless His people for the spread of His grace and glory among all peoples. This will isn't intended to be found; it's intended to be followed. We don't have to wonder about God's will when we've been created to walk in it. We don't need to ask God to reveal His will for our lives.

INSTEAD, WE EACH NEED TO ASK GOD TO ALIGN

OUR LIVES WITH THE WILL HE'S ALREADY REVEALED.

OUR POWER

I know I've spent a lot of time hammering on God's will this week—that He desires to redeem men and women from all people groups throughout the earth, which means He also desires that every disciple of Jesus obey His command to make more disciples of Jesus.

I also realize that by now you've probably moved on to the logical next question: How? As disciples of Jesus, how can we best make other disciples of Jesus among our friends and family, among our neighbors and acquaintances, and among those around the world we've yet to meet? In other words, how do we participate in the fulfillment of God's will?

Surprisingly, the answer to those questions has very little to do with us and very much to do with the Holy Spirit. Indeed, God wants us to experience His will so much that He actually lives inside us in order to accomplish it.

What ideas or images come to mind when you think about the Holy Spirit?

In what ways have you encountered or experienced the Holy Spirit in recent weeks?

As followers of Christ, God unites our lives with the life of Jesus by putting the very Spirit of Jesus inside us. Only through this Spirit do we find the power necessary for making disciples.

Clothed with Power

The end of Luke 24 records Jesus speaking prophetically to His disciples after His death and resurrection:

> **He told them, "This is what is written: The Christ will suffer and rise from the dead on the third day, and repentance and forgiveness of sins will be preached in his name to all nations, beginning at Jerusalem. You are witnesses of these things. I am going to send you what my Father has promised; but stay in the city until you have been clothed with power from on high." Luke 24:46-49**

What strikes you as most interesting in these verses? Why?

This is yet another instance when Jesus proclaimed God's will for the world, but take a moment to focus on that last phrase: "Stay in the city until you have been clothed with power from on high." This is an important point, for God would "clothe," or empower, the disciples to carry out this command by giving them His Holy Spirit. The disciples went on to experience incredible accomplishments, including the launch of the church, but the Holy Spirit fueled everything.

Jesus repeated this idea before His ascension from the Mount of Olives:

> **You will receive power when the Holy Spirit comes on you; and you will be my witnesses in Jerusalem, and in all Judea and Samaria, and to the ends of the earth. Acts 1:8, emphasis added**

Read Acts 2:1-4. How do these verses fulfill Jesus' promises from Luke 24 and Acts 1?

All of these Scripture passages make it clear that a certain kind of power is necessary for us to do the work of making disciples. Both passages also make it clear that we as human beings don't possess this power on our own. It comes from God's Spirit.

Do you rely primarily on your power or on the Holy Spirit in your efforts to live as a follower of Jesus? Explain.

When have you felt empowered by the Holy Spirit to accomplish something? What happened?

As followers of Christ, we have the power of the Spirit of God living in us. Do we realize what that means? Do we realize the unbelievable strength, energy, and life to which we have access?

Just as importantly, do we realize the responsibility that comes with such power?

Called to Proclaim

As followers of Jesus empowered by the Holy Spirit, we have a responsibility to live as witnesses. We have a responsibility to testify about who Jesus is, what Jesus did and continues to do, and how Jesus saves.

What's your reaction to the previous statements? Why?

When have you taken a risk in order to serve as a witness for Jesus? What happened?

Don't minimize the verbal nature of our role as witnesses. We're called to speak. We're called to intentionally seek people who need the truth and then proclaim that truth in a way they can hear and understand.

Interestingly, such an emphasis on verbal speech makes total sense in light of the ways the Holy Spirit operated in the Old Testament. Take a look at the following passages of Scripture to see what I mean.

Read the following verses and record what people did as a result of being filled with the Holy Spirit.

Numbers 11:24-25

2 Chronicles 24:20

Ezekiel 11:5-6

Have you noticed the common element tied to the Holy Spirit in these verses? It's repeated many more times throughout the Bible, including several instances in the New Testament.

Read the following passages of Scripture and record what people did as a result of being filled with the Holy Spirit.

Luke 1:39-45

Acts 4:31

Acts 9:17-20

When the Bible repeats something like this over and over again, in both the Old Testament and the New Testament, we're wise to pay attention. The filling of the Holy Spirit in God's people is clearly linked to a particular purpose: the verbal proclamation of God's Word and the ultimate accomplishment of God's will.

This is exactly what we see Jesus accomplishing through His church in the New Testament. Even though Jesus ascended to heaven in Acts 1, He continued to work by pouring His Spirit on His followers and empowering them to proclaim the gospel.

And Jesus is doing the same thing today. He's filled every one of His followers today with His power and His presence in order to accomplish His purposes in the 21st century. Yet we're prone to miss this, even in the way we talk about the Holy Spirit.

I often hear Christians say, "I share the gospel when the Holy Spirit leads me." There's some truth to that. We want to be led by the Spirit in everything we do. At the same time, we need to remember that the Spirit lives in us for the explicit purpose of spreading the gospel through us.

If you have the Holy Spirit living in you, you can officially consider yourself led to share the gospel! You don't have to wait for a tingly feeling to go down your spine or a special message to appear from heaven before you tell people about Christ. Just open your mouth and talk about the life, death, and resurrection of Jesus, and you'll carry out the purpose of Jesus' presence in you.

Are you aggressive or passive when it comes to sharing the gospel? Explain.

I also hear professing Christians say, "I don't witness with my words; I witness with my life." Again, there's some truth here: we want the character of Christ to be clear in our actions. At the same time, when Jesus told His disciples they'd receive His Spirit and be His witnesses in the world, He wasn't just calling them to be nice to the people around them. Whether in a courtroom or another circumstance, the basic function of a witness is to speak. It's imperative that disciples of Christ speak the truth about the gospel of salvation.

How often do you actively proclaim the gospel in a typical week?

What obstacles prevent you from serving as a witness more often?

God has given us a gospel to believe, a Spirit to empower, and a language to speak for a purpose—a grand, glorious, global, God-exalting purpose that transcends all of history.

DO YOU BELIEVE THIS?

PERSONAL DISCIPLE-MAKING PLAN: HOW TO BE A WITNESS

Because I live in the South, I've noticed that a lot of people get very excited about college football. Specifically, people get very excited about the football teams to which they've attached themselves as fans—the Alabama Crimson Tide, the LSU Tigers, the Georgia Bulldogs, the Tennessee Volunteers, the Ole Miss Rebels, and so on.

People take great pleasure in cheering for their teams and celebrating victories. They go out of their way to extol the many virtues of the team itself as well as the individual players who excel at different positions on the field.

For most fans, however, simple admiration isn't enough. They also spend a tremendous amount of effort trying to prove that their favorite teams and players are better and far more worthy of praise than other teams and players—and that the fans of those other teams and players should switch their allegiance as a result.

This is natural. When we feel deep admiration and appreciation for something, we automatically try to convert—and I use that word intentionally—other people to our way of thinking.

What people, teams, or ideas do you cheer for most intensely? Why?

When have you recently attempted to convince others to cheer for the same thing? What happened?

So here's my question: If we're willing and able to make converts in the name of football teams or movies or books or hobbies, why do we find it so difficult to make disciples of Jesus Christ?

What's your response to the previous question?

God's will in the world and for our lives is to spread His gospel, grace, and glory to all peoples. Instead of asking what God's will is for our lives, every disciple of Jesus asks, "How can my life align with His will for me to be His witness in the world?" This general question leads us to three specific questions: who, how, and when?

Who?

Unlike new converts in Muslim countries, you may not know a lot of people who will kill you because you're a Christian. But I know you're still surrounded by people who aren't Christians.

So take a minute to record the names of 3, 5, or maybe 10 unbelievers God has placed in your life. Then begin praying specifically for God, through the power of His Spirit, to draw each of these people to His salvation.

Who are the people you'll be praying for every day this week?

When and where will you pray for these individuals each day?

For the sake of accountability, whom will you recruit to pray with you each day?

How?

You and I have opportunities to share the gospel every day. In the context of where you live, work, and play and with the people God has put around you (including the names of those you listed above), there are countless chances to speak with someone who isn't a follower of Christ.

I understand you may be afraid. We all have fears that quickly rise to the surface in evangelistic situations—the fear of offending someone, the fear of saying the wrong thing, the fear of being rejected, or just the fear of initiating an awkward conversation.

Yet such fears are only signs that we're forgetting who we are. We're followers of Christ who've been crucified with Him: we no longer live, but Christ lives in us (Gal. 2:20). He's united His life with ours and put His Spirit in us for this purpose. Without Him we have reason to fear; with Him we have reason for faith.

What do you fear most about intentionally sharing the gospel with another person? Why?

How can you increase your confidence in your ability to proclaim the gospel message?

In addition to praying for the salvation of others, I challenge you to pray every morning that God will give you grace as you attempt to proclaim the gospel. Also pray for boldness—for the ability to overcome fear and self-consciousness. Then look intentionally throughout the day for opportunities to share gospel truths. Be ever attentive to situations through which God may open a door for you to share the entire gospel and invite someone to trust in Christ.

What steps can you take to intentionally access the power of the Holy Spirit as you proclaim the gospel?

When?

Instead of passively sitting back and waiting for people to ask you about Jesus, it's wise to consider ways you can actively show His love by creating opportunities to tell people about Him.

Think particularly about the people you'll be praying for each day. How can you specifically and deliberately create opportunities to share the gospel with them? Could you invite them to lunch? Could you have them over for dinner? Is there another activity or avenue you could take advantage of, whether that's something as involved as spending a day or weekend with them or something as simple as writing a letter?

What steps can you take to initiate conversations with the people you'll be praying for each day?

Think about the conversations you'll have this week. What if God has been supernaturally preparing the people on your prayer list for these upcoming conversations? What if He's sovereignly arranged the circumstances in their lives to set the stage for a conversation about Jesus? What if God wants to use you, as you proclaim the gospel, to change their lives forever?

More importantly, what if God desires to accomplish all of those things, yet you choose to remain silent?

Commit to initiating three conversations in the next three days with people from your list. Record which people you'll speak with and how you might initiate each conversation.

1.

2.

3.

As you identify the *who,* think through the *how,* and plan the *when,* don't forget the *why*. All of this can seem fabricated and fake until you remember what's at stake. Every person God has graciously put around you is a sinner eternally in need of a Savior. You were once that person, yet someone intentionally sought you to share the gospel with you. And now this is the purpose for which God has graciously saved you.

WITH THE WORD OF GOD IN YOUR MOUTH AND THE SPIRIT

OF GOD IN YOUR HEART, END YOUR QUEST TO FIND

GOD'S WILL BY DECIDING TO FOLLOW IT EVEN TODAY.

THE CHURCH

Welcome back to this group discussion of *Follow Me*.

Last week's application activity involved carrying a blank piece of paper with you each day to remind you to give God a blank check with your life. If you're comfortable, share what you found interesting or enlightening about that experience.

On a practical level, what it does it look like for Christians to offer God a blank check with their lives? What does that mean in terms of attitudes and actions?

Describe what you liked best about the study material in week 4. What questions do you have?

What emotions do you experience when you hear the following terms?

• *Church*

• *Accountability*

• *Church membership*

• *Church discipline*

To prepare to view the DVD segment, read aloud Ephesians 4:1-6:

> **As a prisoner for the Lord, then, I urge you to live a life worthy of the calling you have received. Be completely humble and gentle; be patient, bearing with one another in love. Make every effort to keep the unity of the Spirit through the bond of peace. There is one body and one Spirit—just as you were called to one hope when you were called—one Lord, one faith, one baptism; one God and Father of all, who is over all and through all and in all.**

WATCH

Complete the viewer guide below as you watch DVD session 5.

You cannot be a devoted disciple of Christ and you cannot fully make disciples of Christ apart from total _____ to a local church.

Why people minimize the church: we're _____, we're _____, we're _____, we're _____, and we're _____.

God's Word says _____ in the local church is extremely important.

God's Word helps us see the importance of church _____.

The local church is a visible _____ of the universal body of Christ.

God's Word helps us see the importance of church _____.

God's Word helps us see the importance of church _____.

God's Word helps us see the importance of church _____.

Baptism is a declaration that we belong to _____.

Baptism is a declaration that we belong to _____ _____.

Together in the church, we want to know the _____ of Christ.

Together in the church, we want to imitate the _____ of Christ.

Together in the church, we want to display the _____ of Christ.

The local church is a local body of _____ believers joined together under biblical leadership to grow in the likeness of Christ and _____ the love of Christ to each other and to the world around them.

_____ is the distinguishing mark of the church.

Discuss the DVD segment with your group, using the questions below.

What did you like best from David's teaching? Why?

Respond to David's statement: "You can't be a devoted disciple of Christ and you can't fully make disciples of Christ apart from total commitment to a church."

As a group, summarize David's teaching on the four terms discussed earlier:

• *Church*

• *Accountability*

• *Church membership*

• *Church discipline*

What policies has your church adopted on church membership? Church discipline?

Respond to David's definition of a local church: "The church is a local body of baptized believers joined together under biblical leadership to grow in the likeness of Christ and to express the love of Christ to one another and to the world around them."

How have you experienced love as a member of a local church?

Application: Commit to gaining a better understanding of your local church this week. Read material on your church's Web site and your church's statement of beliefs, interview staff members, attend one or more activities you've not yet experienced, and so on.

Scripture: Memorize Ephesians 4:15-16 this week.

READ week 5 and complete the activities before the next group experience.
READ chapter 7 in the book *Follow Me* by David Platt (Tyndale, 2013).

Speaking the truth in love, we will in all things grow up into him who is the Head, that is, Christ. From him the whole body, joined and held together by every supporting ligament, grows and builds itself up in love, as each part does its work. Ephesians 4:15-16

So far in this study we've explored several different aspects of what it means to live as a follower of Christ.

We've looked at both the costs and the rewards connected with Jesus' call to follow Him. We've seen the differences between superficial religion and supernatural regeneration. We've explored how following Jesus transforms us from the inside out, changing our thoughts, our desires, our will, our relationships, and our entire purpose for living. We've gained a better understanding of what it means to delight in Christ, and we've built a better perspective on how to identify and obey God's will.

You may have noticed, however, that we haven't spent much time discussing the institution most commonly associated with those who choose to follow Christ: the church. We haven't yet explored what it means for a follower of Christ to participate in the body of Christ.

It's time for us to dive into that exploration, and I couldn't be more excited. Why? Because it's a privilege to be part of the church.

To come to Christ is to become a part of His church. As men and women die to themselves and live in Christ, God brings them together as brothers and sisters in a family of faith. This community of Christians regularly worships with one another, selflessly serves one another, graciously guards one another, generously gives to one another, and compassionately cares for one another.

Who wouldn't be excited about being a member of that kind of community?

THE CHURCH

MODERN MISCONCEPTIONS

The room was packed full of people, and the preacher held his audience in the palm of his hand. "I'd like everyone to bow your heads and close your eyes," he said. We did so, and he continued, "Tonight I want to call you to put your faith in God. Tonight I'm urging you to begin a personal relationship with Jesus for the first time in your life."

"Let me be clear," the preacher said. "I'm not inviting you to join the church. I'm just inviting you to come to Christ." As he passionately pleaded for personal decisions, scores of people stood from their seats and walked down the aisles of the auditorium to make a commitment to Christ.

I felt conflicted as I watched the scene unfold. Certainly I was glad to see so many people responding to the convicting work of the Holy Spirit. I rejoiced to see men and women moved to the point of taking public action to express their desire to follow Christ.

Yet there was a problem, and it made me feel uneasy in spite of the positive atmosphere in the auditorium. The people walking down the aisles had been deceived. They'd been told it's possible to make a commitment to Christ apart from a commitment to the church—something I knew to be untrue.

Here's the reality: it's biblically impossible to follow Christ apart from joining His church. In fact, anyone who claims to be a Christian yet isn't an active member of a church may not actually be a follower of Christ at all.

What's your reaction to the previous statements? Why?

To some, the previous statements may sound heretical. "Are you saying that joining a church makes someone a Christian?" Absolutely not. Joining a church most certainly doesn't make someone a Christian.

At the same time, to identify your life with the Person of Christ is to join your life with the people of Christ. To surrender your life to His commands is to commit your life to His church. It's biblically, spiritually, and practically impossible to be a disciple of Christ (much less *make* disciples of Christ) apart from total devotion to a family of Christians.

Describe your current involvement in a local church.

How has your connection to the church empowered you to live as a disciple of Christ and to work toward making more disciples of Christ?

A Poor Reputation

Let's be honest: many people consider *church* to be a four-letter word—they say "church" in the same way they might spit out a curse. These men and women do everything they can to avoid entering a church building, and they're often openly antagonistic toward people who choose to do so every week.

Such people have existed for as long as Christians have been living and ministering in the world. In fact, Jesus warned us about them during His public ministry:

> **If the world hates you, keep in mind that it hated me first. If you belonged to the world, it would love you as its own. As it is, you do not belong to the world, but I have chosen you out of the world. That is why the world hates you. Remember the words I spoke to you: "No servant is greater than his master." If they persecuted me, they will persecute you also. John 15:18-20**

Why do many people in today's society feel antagonistic toward Christians and the church?

When have you experienced oppression or hostility because of your decision to follow Jesus?

Jesus promised that the world would hate His followers; therefore, we should never be surprised when people from the world choose to hate the church. What should surprise us, however—what certainly surprises me—is the number of Christians who've chosen to set themselves against the body of Christ.

You've probably heard modern Christians expressing distaste for the church. Indeed, in some circles it's become a mark of spiritual maturity for professing Christians to *avoid* becoming active in a local church. "I love Jesus," these people say, "but I just can't stand the church."

Here's my question: Isn't the church the bride of Christ? What if I said to you, "Man, I love you, but have I ever told you how much I can't stand your wife?" Would you take it as a compliment?

Similarly, the church is the body of Christ. What if my wife said to me, "David, I love you, but I can't stand your body"? I can assure you that I wouldn't take that as a compliment!

What images or ideas come to mind when you hear the word *church?*

How have your experiences with church been confusing or frustrating?

Here's the truth: it's impossible to follow Jesus fully without loving His bride selflessly, and it's impossible to think we can enjoy Christ apart from His body.

A Poor Definition

There are a number of reasons people feel negative about the church. Probably the most common reason occurs when Christians and non-Christians feel they've been wronged or treated unfairly by individual followers of Jesus, which leads them to project those negative experiences onto the church as a whole.

This is more than unfortunate, especially since Christians have been given commands such as this one from Ephesians 4:

> **As a prisoner for the Lord, then, I urge you to live a life worthy of the calling you have received. Be completely humble and gentle; be patient, bearing with one another in love. Make every effort to keep the unity of the Spirit through the bond of peace. Ephesians 4:1-3**

How do you measure up to the standards listed in these verses? Explain.

But I also think people choose to dislike the church because they've formed a poor definition of what the church actually is. And sadly, I fear Christians are largely at fault for producing these definitions. In the same way we've diluted what it means to be a Christian in today's world, we've also skewed what it means to be a church.

For example, the majority of people in Western culture associate the concept of church with a physical building. "Where is your church?" people may ask or "Where do you go to church?" Construction teams of Christians travel overseas to impoverished countries in order to build "churches." Planting a church in our day has become almost synonymous with finding or erecting a building.

Why is it inaccurate to think of churches primarily in terms of physical buildings?

What are the practical consequences of this misconception?

We not only identify buildings as churches; we also classify churches according to the programs they offer. "This church has a creative children's program," we say, or "That church has great resources for married couples." More and more, church life is expected to revolve around programs offered for every age and stage of life.

Both of these misconceptions reflect an overtly consumer-driven, customer-designed approach we've devised for attracting people to church. We think in order for church to be successful, we need an accessible building with nice grounds and convenient parking. Once people get to the building, we need programs that are customized for people's children, music that's attractive to people's tastes, and sermons that are aimed at people's needs.

But is that what God had in mind when He set up His church? Better yet, is *any* of this what God had in mind when He set up His church? We'll explore those questions tomorrow.

IN DOING SO, WE'LL GAIN A BETTER UNDERSTANDING

OF WHAT THE CHURCH IS SUPPOSED TO BE.

WHAT IS THE CHURCH?

Let's get started today by reviewing a couple of vocabulary words. Specifically, let's take a deeper look at two terms that are useful when contemplating the proper interpretation of God's Word: *extrabiblical* and *unbiblical*.

The term *extrabiblical* refers to something that's outside the truth of God's Word—something that's often connected to the Bible but doesn't have its source in the Bible. So an extrabiblical concept may be interesting, even helpful, but it's not a purely biblical concept; it doesn't carry the authority of Scripture. For example, Josephus was an ancient historian who lived and wrote during the time of Jesus, but he's not directly connected to the Bible. His writings are extrabiblical sources.

The term *unbiblical* refers to something that undercuts the truth of God's Word—a concept or idea that disagrees with the testimony of the Bible. For example, "God helps those who help themselves" is an unbiblical statement.

In your own words, explain the difference between the terms *extrabiblical* and *unbiblical*.

Why am I emphasizing the meanings of these terms? Because we're talking about modern conceptions and expressions of the church. And sadly, much of what we associate with the church today is extrabiblical at best and unbiblical at worst.

For example, the identification of churches with buildings may seem common to us, but it's foreign to the New Testament, where we never once see the church described as a physical building. Similarly, the New Testament never once portrays the church as a conglomeration of customized programs.

Instead, the New Testament defines the church with imagery that's both powerful and intimate. The church is defined as the body of Christ, both local and universal, and as a community of believers.

The Church Is a Body

Throughout the New Testament, the church is described as a body in which Christians are parts, or members. Look at 1 Corinthians 12, for example:

> **The body is a unit, though it is made up of many parts; and though all its parts are many, they form one body. So it is with Christ. For we were all baptized by one Spirit into one body—whether Jews or Greeks, slave or free—and we were all given the one Spirit to drink. Now you are the body of Christ, and each one of you is a part of it. 1 Corinthians 12:12-13,27**

What do find encouraging in these verses? Why?

Read 1 Corinthians 12:14-26. Describe the primary theme of these verses in one sentence.

I know you've probably heard the term *body of Christ* thousands of times before, but Paul's imagery in these verses is shocking. He was describing the church as a living, physical organism—something that contains a myriad of different parts and yet works together in perfect harmony in order to live and move and breathe.

Do we realize the depth of intimacy implied by that image? Paul recognized that the church is made up of individual human beings, but he didn't imply we can all have individual goals, desires, and motivations. No, we move together under a unified, collective will—God's will. All of our individual efforts are swept up into a larger body that must work together in order to survive.

Look at verses 25-26: "... so that there should be no division in the body, but that its parts should have equal concern for each other. If one part suffers, every part suffers with it; if one part is honored, every part rejoices with it." The body of Christ is a picture of extreme intimacy and unity of purpose.

In what ways does the church today demonstrate unity and teamwork?

In what ways does the church today demonstrate disunity and a lack of common purpose?

Read 1 Corinthians 12:14-20. What's required from us as individuals in order to maintain unity in the body of Christ?

The Church Is Local and Universal

When we describe the church as the body of Christ, we typically use that term in reference to the universal church—the global body of Christ made up of all Christians around the world. And that's true. Whenever we come to faith in Christ, we join followers of Christ all over the world and throughout all history.

Do you feel connected to the universal body of Christ? Explain.

But we need to understand that the church is both universal *and* local. Yes, there are many passages of Scripture such as Ephesians 1:22 that provide a universal picture of the church. But there are far more passages of Scripture that reference local church gatherings.

In fact, of the 114 times the word *ekklesia (church)* is used in the New Testament, at least 90 of those uses refer to specific local gatherings of believers. Acts 11:22 mentions "the church at Jerusalem," for example. The Book of 1 Corinthians is addressed "to the church of God in Corinth" (1:2). Romans 16:5 refers to "the church that meets at [Priscilla and Aquila's] house."

Notice these references aren't directed at parts or segments of the church. Paul never wrote "to the part of the church that meets in Corinth." Instead, he wrote "to the church of God in Corinth," demonstrating to us all throughout the New Testament that believers are joined together in local bodies of Christ that are tangible, visible expressions of the universal body of Christ.

What do you like best about your local church?

How does your local church help you experience the global body of Christ?

So when the New Testament talks about the church, we see two different pictures: (1) the universal body of Christ made up of all true believers throughout history and (2) local gatherings of believers on earth who worship together, minister with one another, and love one another.

The Church Is a Community

Biblically, a church doesn't consist of people who simply show up, park, and participate in programs alongside one another. Instead, the church is composed of people who share the life of Christ with one another on a day-by-day, week-by-week basis.

This was the pattern set between Jesus and His disciples from the beginning. Jesus loved those 12 men, served them, taught them, encouraged them, corrected them, and journeyed through life with them. He spent more time with those 12 disciples than He did with everyone else in His ministry put together.

During all this time together, Jesus taught His disciples how to live and showed them how to love as He shared His life with them.

What opportunities do you currently have to share life with other Christians?

In the same way, the New Testament envisions followers of Jesus living alongside one another for the sake of one another. The Bible portrays the church as a community of Christians who care for one another, love one another, host one another, receive one another, honor one another, serve one another, instruct one another, forgive one another, motivate one another, build up one another, encourage one another, comfort one another, pray for one another, confess sin to one another, esteem one another, edify one another, teach one another, show kindness to one another, give to one another, rejoice with one another, weep with one another, hurt with one another, and restore one another.

All of these "one anothers," combined together, paint a picture not of people who come to a building filled with customized programs but of people who've decided to lay down their lives to love one another.

What's your reaction to the previous statements? Why?

Read the following passages of Scripture and record what each teaches about the way Christians are to interact as members of the same body.

Romans 12:9-13

Ephesians 4:25-32

1 Thessalonians 5:12-15

What is the church? It's the body of Christ living and active in today's world.

IT'S A COMMUNITY OF CHRISTIANS WHO LOVE ONE ANOTHER AND LONG FOR ONE ANOTHER TO KNOW AND GROW IN JESUS.

CHURCH DISCIPLINE

I was eating lunch with a fellow pastor a while ago and happened to share that we were trying to implement a process for church discipline and restoration in the church I pastor. He said to me, "I'd love to hear how that goes. Give me a call in a few weeks if you're still there." Well, by God's grace I'm still here. And though the church I pastor has a long way to go in fully implementing this process, I'm more firmly convinced than ever that such discipline and restoration are essential for every disciple of Christ and every church that claims His name.

What ideas or images come to mind when you hear the term *church discipline?*

When have you seen church discipline put into practice by a local gathering of believers? What happened?

I understand that many Christians don't react positively to the concept of church discipline. I also understand that, when handled wrongly, the practice can become legalistic and create a lot of damage. But please hear me on this: when handled biblically, church discipline and restoration are two of the clearest expressions of God's love on earth.

What Jesus Taught

You may find this interesting: in the Gospels Jesus talked with His disciples specifically about the church on only two occasions. The first time is in Matthew 16, when Peter confessed Jesus as the Christ. In response Jesus proclaimed that the church would be built on that confession—on the recognition that Jesus is "the Christ, the Son of the living God" (v. 16).

Jesus' only other instructions about the church come two chapters later. Surprisingly, those instructions deal with church discipline and restoration. According to Jesus, when a brother or a sister is wandering into sin, caught in sin, or unrepentant in sin, the church should confront that person and pull him or her back to Christ. Jesus outlined a process for such restoration—one that eventually leads to removing unrepentant sinners from the church altogether, if necessary.

Read Matthew 18:15-17. What emotions do you experience when you read these verses? Why?

Can this process be carried out in the church today? Explain.

Jesus' teaching on church discipline and restoration should jump off the pages of Scripture and grab our attention. This wasn't number 100 on a list of 101 things Jesus said we should do as His people. This was at the *top* of the list, right after the importance of confessing Him as Lord.

In other words, church discipline isn't a supplemental practice for Christians; it's fundamental. Church discipline isn't optional; it's essential.

What's your reaction to the previous statements? Why?

Unfortunately, Christians and churches today treat church discipline and restoration as if they were optional. We tell ourselves church discipline is legalistic; it contradicts God's grace. We think of Matthew 7:1, where Jesus said, "Do not judge, or you too will be judged." We live in a day when it's easy, even preferred, for people to sit back and say, "What other people do is between them and God. Their sin is their life, their decision, and their responsibility."

But aren't you glad this isn't the way God responds to you? Aren't you glad God pursues you despite your sin and pulls you away from the things that would destroy you? And don't you want people in your life who love you enough to look out for you when you begin to walk down a road of sinful destruction?

When has another person helped you avoid making a major mistake? How do you feel about that person now?

Believe me, helping someone escape the power of sin isn't judgmental; it's an extreme act of love.

An Act of Love

Dietrich Bonhoeffer once said, "Nothing can be more cruel than the tenderness that consigns another to his sin. Nothing can be more compassionate than the severe rebuke that calls a brother back from the path of sin."[1] That's the heart of church discipline and restoration. God is a gracious Father who seeks His wandering children, and we reflect His grace when we care for brothers and sisters who are caught in sin.

Do you agree with the previous statements? Explain.

How do your actions and relationships reflect your opinion of those statements?

Look at the way the apostle James concluded his epistle to the early church:

> **My brothers, if one of you should wander from the truth and someone should bring him back, remember this: Whoever turns a sinner from the error of his way will save him from death and cover over a multitude of sins. James 5:19-20**

What obstacles prevent you from actively working to pull your friends and family away from sin?

Clearly, there's value in being willing to help those who are wandering from the truth. At the same time, we must remember that *we* need help as well. We need to seek people who love us enough to point out *our* sins if we're going to live as followers of Jesus—and we must be willing to listen.

I know I have blind spots in my life, and I know I'm prone to sin. That's why I've told the people closest to me, "If you see me walking into sin, caught in sin, or being pulled into sin, please don't use superspiritual jargon as an excuse for not helping me. Pull me back!"

Read 1 Corinthians 5:1-13. What problem was Paul addressing in these verses?

Summarize Paul's commands in verses 9-11. What's your reaction to those commands?

What's particularly interesting in 1 Corinthians 5 is the way God holds the members of the church accountable for the man's sinful relationship. Certainly, the members of the church weren't accountable for committing the sexual immorality, but they *were* accountable for not addressing it in their midst.

This teaching clearly goes completely against the grain of the way we think today. We take a much more individualistic approach to sin. "That sin is that brother's problem," we say to one another and ourselves. But that's exactly what the church at Corinth was saying, and Paul rebuked them for it. This man's sin was that church's problem.

This reality is central to understanding the beauty of biblical, Christ-centered community. In the church we belong to one another and care for one another in such a way that we're responsible for one another. Being a member of a church means realizing we're responsible for helping the brothers and sisters around us grow as disciples of Jesus. And they're responsible for helping us. We desperately need one another in the daily fight to follow Christ in a world that's full of sin.

When have you seen one person's continued sin affect the community of a local church?

Maybe you're wondering, *Won't some people leave the church (or avoid the church altogether) if we start practicing discipline the way Jesus talks about?* Possibly, but we need to remember that the church is Christ's body to grow, not ours.

For far too long we've ignored passages like Matthew 18, Acts 5, and 1 Corinthians 5, pretending that our catchphrases and creative programs are more effective means for drawing people to the church. As a result, the credit for growth in contemporary Christianity often goes to the most pioneering pastor with the most innovative church and the most appealing worship service. That's a problem.

IT'S HIGH TIME FOR THIS TO CHANGE SO THAT CREDIT FOR GROWTH IN THE CHURCH CAN GO ONLY TO THE GREAT AND HOLY GOD OF THE UNIVERSE WHO DISPLAYS HIS GLORY BY INEXPLICABLY DRAWING SINNERS TO HIMSELF THROUGH THE PURITY OF PEOPLE WHO'VE BEEN BOUGHT BY HIS BLOOD.

CHURCH MEMBERSHIP

When I was a junior in high school, I hadn't had much success on the relationship front. Truth be told, I hadn't had *any* success on the relationship front—until a certain girl came to a camp I attended. Word got around that she thought I was cute. A little while later, we started dating, which consisted of talking on the phone every day and spending time together in different settings.

Everything was going well until one very bad night. I decided I wasn't up to talking on the phone every day any longer; in fact, I decided I didn't really want to work on the relationship any longer. So I told this girl that I had a lot of things going on in my life. I told her that God, my family, and my schoolwork were more important to me than she was.

Yes, my *schoolwork*. Needless to say, my first dating experience didn't last very long.

What emotions do you experience when you hear the word *dating?* Why?

Describe a few of your favorite memories from dating experiences.

Thankfully, I had later opportunities to get to know this girl all over again. In fact, things got to the point that we eventually became best friends and decided to get married. Ever since that conversation on that bad night many years ago, my bride has proved to be more than patient with me.

Why do I bring up this story? Because a trend has developed in Christian culture that's often referred to as dating the church. In our consumer-driven church market, we've developed the practice of hopping from one church to the next, attending this church or that church based on how we feel on a particular Sunday morning or maybe just leaning on "spiritual" activities and not attending church at all.

After all, we're Christians. We're a part of the church around the world—the global body of Christ. So why do we need to commit to a local church?

The answer to that question has everything to do with the value of church membership in our continuing efforts to live as followers of Christ.

What does it mean to be a member of a local church?

Are you currently a member of a local church? Explain why or why not.

Why We Date the Church

The basic idea behind dating the church is a desire to avoid committing ourselves to a specific body of believers. And there are a variety of reasons so many Christians wish to avoid such a commitment.

For one thing, most Christians living in Western culture are independent, self-reliant, self-sufficient people. Therefore, the thought of mutual submission, accountability, and interdependence seems foreign to us—if not outright frightening.

What's your reaction to the previous statements? Why?

In addition, we're indecisive. We date different churches because we can't decide on the one we really like. It's a consumer mentality applied to church shopping—looking for the best product with the best price on Sunday morning. We're always looking for the better deal, which often leads to a fairly critical attitude toward the church. We can find something wrong with every church we visit, and even when we settle down somewhere, we're ever cognizant of the things we don't like.

On the whole we're often indifferent. Is joining and committing to a local church really that big a deal? Isn't it just a formality and an unnecessary formality at that? Many professing Christians simply have no idea why dating the church would be wrong and why devotion to the church would be necessary.

What process did you follow before choosing the church you currently attend?

How would you describe your level of commitment to your current church? Explain.

When we dig deeper into the issues surrounding church membership, we find that it's not only important from a biblical perspective; it also provides great benefits to those of us who choose to follow Christ.

The Value of Church Membership

Sometimes it's easy for us to miss the way the New Testament expresses the value of church membership, because the concept of church membership is almost always assumed or implied by the biblical authors.

For example, we talked earlier this week about the importance of local churches as visible expressions of the universal body of Christ. When you think about it, however, local churches can't exist without church membership. There could have been no "church of God in Corinth" (1 Cor. 1:2) if individual Christians hadn't committed to join together as a local body in that region. The same is true of the churches in Rome, Ephesus, Antioch, Thessalonica, and so on. These local gatherings would have had no significance if the early Christians had thought of themselves only as members of the global body of Christ.

Indeed, it's significant that we never see the New Testament addressing followers of Christ who didn't belong to a local church. That fact speaks volumes about the value of church membership.

In your own words, what's the connection between church membership and the continued existence of local churches?

The value of church membership is also assumed when the New Testament describes the need for and the process of church discipline.

Look again at Matthew 18:15-20 and 1 Corinthians 5:1-13. What are the different steps involved in church discipline?

Notice Jesus' reference to "the church" (Matt. 18:17). Jesus certainly wasn't saying that if a believer continues unrepentant in sin, then his sin should be told to the universal body of Christ around the world. Instead, Jesus was referring to a specific local body of believers of which that brother was a part—a member.

Likewise, when Paul addressed the unrepentant brother in the church at Corinth, he said, "Expel the wicked man from among you" (1 Cor. 5:13). Paul was talking about removing a brother from the church, which has obvious implications for church membership. To be a Christian and yet unattached to a local church was a big deal. It was a form of punishment designed to help the Christian repent of sin. Therefore, this isn't a state we should voluntarily seek.

What would change in your life if you were involuntarily removed from your local church?

The importance of every Christian's being a member of a church is also clear when the Bible talks about church leadership. Hebrews 13 commands Christians:

> **Obey your leaders and submit to their authority. They keep watch over you as men who must give an account. Obey them so that their work will be a joy, not a burden, for that would be of no advantage to you. Hebrews 13:17**

What's your reaction to this verse? Why?

This verse illustrates the importance of church membership on two different levels. For church leaders, it's a reminder that God has entrusted certain believers into their care in a local church. Indeed, this verse reminds me personally that I'm accountable before God for the Christians He's entrusted me to pastor. So whom does that include? Am I accountable to God for the care of every single follower of Jesus in the universal body of Christ? Thankfully, no.

Similarly, from a Christian's perspective, Hebrews 13:17 commands followers of Christ to obey their leaders. Does this mean every Christian is accountable to follow the direction of every Christian leader in the universal body of Christ? Surely not. This is a specific command for Christians to follow leaders in the local church of which they're a part.

And make no mistake: this command is for your benefit as a member of a local church. I know there have been times when leaders have abused their positions in the church, but that's never been part of God's design. In addition, those instances of poor leadership don't negate the overwhelming benefits of godly leadership in the local church.

Read the following passages of Scripture and record the benefits church members receive from their leaders.

Acts 20:25-31

Hebrews 13:7

1 Peter 5:1-4

When have you been blessed by the leaders of your church?

So is it a good thing for you and me to commit to a church under the leadership of pastors who faithfully teach God's Word and consistently model God's character? Absolutely. According to Scripture, it's necessary.

THIS IS GOD'S GOOD DESIGN FOR EVERY DISCIPLE OF JESUS.

PERSONAL DISCIPLE-MAKING PLAN: HOW TO BE A CHURCH MEMBER

We've looked at the church from a variety of angles this week. I'd like to finish this discussion with a quick exploration of several verses in Ephesians 4. This is a wonderful passage of Scripture that helps us think deeply about the importance of the local church in our everyday lives.

First, look at verses 2-6:

> **Be completely humble and gentle; be patient, bearing with one another in love. Make every effort to keep the unity of the Spirit through the bond of peace. There is one body and one Spirit—just as you were called to one hope when you were called—one Lord, one faith, one baptism; one God and Father of all, who is over all and through all and in all.**

What strikes you as most interesting in these verses? Why?

Verses 5-6 describe the presence of "one Lord, one faith, one baptism; one God and Father of all." How do these realities create unity in the church?

One of Paul's goals in these verses was to show church members that we belong not only to Jesus but also to one another. We all come from different backgrounds, and we all have different personalities, but we form one church. That's another reason baptism is such a powerful symbol. It's something that links all followers of Jesus and points to our mutual death and new life.

Read Ephesians 4:11-13. What do these verses teach about leaders in the church?

According to these verses, what responsibilities do church leaders carry?

Toward what goals should we be working as church members?

Finally, look at verses 14-16:

> **Then we will no longer be infants, tossed back and forth by the waves, and blown here and there by every wind of teaching and by the cunning and craftiness of men in their deceitful scheming. Instead, speaking the truth in love, we will in all things grow up into him who is the Head, that is, Christ. From him the whole body, joined and held together by every supporting ligament, grows and builds itself up in love, as each part does its work.**

Notice that love is the distinguishing mark of the church. We speak the truth in love. We build up one another in love. Ultimately, why should we join a church? Because of love. Jesus taught that love is the essence of church membership: "By this all men will know that you are my disciples, if you love one another" (John 13:35).

In what ways have you recently experienced love as a member of the church?

In what ways have you recently expressed love as a member of the church?

Keeping in mind Ephesians 4 and everything we've explored this week, here's my best shot at a definition of the local church: *the church is a local body of baptized believers joined together under biblical leadership to grow in the likeness of Christ and to express the love of Christ to one another and to the world around them.*

Don't you want to be part of that kind of community? Who would turn up their nose at the opportunity to participate in something that magnificent? Not me. And I hope you wouldn't either.

So the question becomes: Have you been participating in that kind of church? And if not, what can be done about it? I encourage you to examine yourself and your commitment to the church by answering three important questions.

Are You Committed to a Local Church?

This is the question we must ask ourselves to begin our self-examination: *Am I an active, accountable member of a local church?* Notice that the question isn't simply, *Is my name on a church-membership list somewhere?* Nor is it, *Do I attend a church somewhere?*

No, the real question is this: *Am I committed to a local church where I'm sharing life with other followers of Christ in mutual accountability under biblical leadership for the glory of God?*

What's your answer to the previous question?

Record your recent experiences with each component of that question.

How have you recently shared your life with other followers of Christ in mutual accountability?

How have you experienced biblical leadership in your church?

How have you been empowered and encouraged to glorify God as a member of your church?

According to the New Testament, if you're casually dating (or altogether ignoring) the local church, you're living in a way that's contrary to God's design for your life as a Christian. It's impossible to follow Christ apart from commitment to a local church.

If you're not satisfied with your answers to the previous questions, you need to ask yourself another question.

Where Should You Commit?

Throughout the year the church I pastor hosts a four-week class for potential church members. During that time I always say the same thing to every person in the class: "Is this the local body of Christ where you can most effectively make disciples of Christ?"

If the answer to that question is yes, then I encourage them to lock arms with our local church, not as spectators on the sidelines but as participants in the mission. If the answer to that question is no, then I encourage them to lock arms with another local church where they can more effectively carry out the commission of Christ.

What about you?

Where is the place where you can most effectively make disciples of all nations?

Where are the pastors you can confidently follow because they clearly teach and model God's Word?

Where are the people you'll commit to serve and submit to as a disciple of Jesus?

Answering these questions and committing your life to a church then lead to a final question.

How Will You Serve as a Member of the Church?

As you think about the church of which you're a member, consider what you can do to build up and be built up by that body of Christ. Are there certain people you can serve in specific ways? Are there certain positions you can fill for specific purposes? What will you do to lay down your life for the people of that church? And what will you do to make sure you have people who are watching out for your life in Christ, willing to pull you back when you start to wander from Him?

Which people in your local church have needs you're capable of meeting?

In what ways are you currently serving your local church? What fruit has been generated by that service?

In what other ways could you contribute as a member of your church? Whom can you consult with to decide whether you should increase your service?

To follow Christ is to love His church. It's biblically, spiritually, and practically impossible to be a disciple of Christ, much less make disciples of Christ, apart from total devotion to a family of Christians.

HOW WILL YOUR LIFE BE SPENT SHOWING

GOD'S LOVE AS A MEMBER OF A CHURCH?

1. Dietrich Bonhoeffer, *Life Together* (New York: Harper & Row, 1954), 107.

WEEK 6
OUR MISSION

Welcome back to this group discussion of *Follow Me*.

Last week's application activity challenged you to gain a greater understanding of your local church. Discuss what you found most interesting and impactful.

What do you appreciate most about your local church? Why?

Describe what you liked best about the study material in week 5. What questions do you have?

Which individuals currently have authority over your daily life? How do you typically react when they assert that authority?

To prepare to view the DVD segment, read aloud Matthew 28:16-20:

> **The eleven disciples went to Galilee, to the mountain where Jesus had told them to go. When they saw him, they worshiped him; but some doubted. Then Jesus came to them and said, "All authority in heaven and on earth has been given to me. Therefore go and make disciples of all nations, baptizing them in the name of the Father and of the Son and of the Holy Spirit, and teaching them to obey everything I have commanded you. And surely I am with you always, to the very end of the age."**

Complete the viewer guide below as you watch DVD session 6.

As disciples of Jesus, let's _____ in the authority of Christ.

Jesus is the _____ Lord and Savior over all.

Jesus has authority over _____ life.

Jesus' authority _____ us to go.

Jesus' authority gives us _____ as we go.

As disciples of Jesus, let's _____ the command of Christ.

Every follower of Jesus is a _____ of men.

Every _____ is a disciple maker.

How do we make disciples? We _____ and we share the Word.

We share the Word, and then we _____ the Word.

Every Christian will _____ in their relationship with Christ until they begin to give their life for the sake of others through disciple making.

We _____ the Word.

We _____ the world.

As we make disciples of all nations, we will multiply _____ among all nations.

As disciples of Jesus, let's _____ on the presence of Christ.

This _____ is not based on who we are or what we can do; this _____ is based on who Jesus is and what He is able to do in and through our lives.

Video sessions available for purchase at *www.lifeway.com/followme*

Discuss the DVD segment with your group, using the questions below.

What did you like best from David's teaching? Why?

Why is it important that Jesus claimed all authority in heaven and on earth?

In what ways did Jesus demonstrate His authority during His public ministry?

Respond to David's statement: "Matthew 28:19 is not a comfortable call for most Christians to come, be baptized, and sit in one location. This is a costly command for every Christian to go, baptize, and make disciples of all nations. Every Christian."

What steps have you personally taken to serve the nations and proclaim the gospel to all peoples? What steps would you like to take in the coming year?

When have you recently been supported and empowered by Christ's presence in your daily life? How did you react to His presence?

What steps can you take to increase your dependence on the presence of Christ?

Application: David said, "Let's be a part of something that is beyond us. Let's be a part of something where we need His presence. Let's not be Christians in churches filled with programs and practices that we can manage on our own." As you pray throughout this week, ask Jesus to give you a goal or vision that can be accomplished only through His power and presence in your life. Commit to consistently and persistently pray for that goal or vision. Also pray that Jesus will truly be with you as you seek to follow Him.

Scripture: Memorize Matthew 28:18-20 this week.

READ week 6 and complete the activities to conclude this study.
READ chapters 8–9 in the book *Follow Me* by David Platt (Tyndale, 2013).

This Week's Scripture Memory

Jesus came to them and said, "All authority in heaven and on earth has been given to me. Therefore go and make disciples of all nations, baptizing them in the name of the Father and of the Son and of the Holy Spirit, and teaching them to obey everything I have commanded you. And surely I am with you always, to the very end of the age." Matthew 28:18-20

What do you want in life? What do you hope to experience as a follower of Christ? What do you hope to find as a member of the church?

I'll tell you what I want: I want to be a part of a people who really believe we have the Spirit of God in us for the spread of the gospel through all of us. I want to be a part of a people who are gladly sacrificing the pleasures, pursuits, and possessions of this world because we're living for treasure in the world to come. I want to be a part of a people who've forsaken every earthly ambition in favor of one eternal aspiration: to see disciples made and churches multiplied from our houses to our communities to our cities and the nations.

This kind of movement involves all of us. It involves every disciple making disciples—no more spectators. It involves ordinary people spreading the gospel in extraordinary ways all over the world. It involves men and women from diverse backgrounds with different gifts and distinct platforms making disciples and multiplying churches through every domain of society in every place on the planet.

This is God's design for His church, and disciples of Jesus mustn't settle for anything less.

Who can imagine or measure what might happen when all of the people of God begin to prayerfully, humbly, simply, and intentionally make disciples? What if every one of us as followers of Christ really started fishing for men? This is *the* way God has designed for His unfathomable grace to spread to the ends of the earth in order to achieve His ultimate glory. And this is *the* life God has ordained for every child of His—to enjoy His grace as we extend His glory to every group of people in the world.

What about you? As we finish this study together, what do you want?

OUR MISSION

DAY 1
BELIEVE THE AUTHORITY
OF CHRIST

We began this study by exploring the first words Jesus spoke to His disciples in the Gospel of Matthew: " 'Come, follow me,' Jesus said, 'and I will make you fishers of men' " (4:19). That was the call that changed the lives of the four men who heard it and followed.

I think it's appropriate, then, to end this study by exploring the last words Jesus spoke to His disciples in the Gospel of Matthew. We usually refer to those words as the Great Commission:

> **Jesus came to them and said, "All authority in heaven and on earth has been given to me. Therefore go and make disciples of all nations, baptizing them in the name of the Father and of the Son and of the Holy Spirit, and teaching them to obey everything I have commanded you. And surely I am with you always, to the very end of the age." Matthew 28:18-20**

What commands did Jesus give His disciples in these verses?

How did Jesus encourage His disciples in these verses?

These verses are familiar to most Christians, and they should serve as the driving force behind every decision in our lives. Yet so often we forget to heed them. Tragically, the Great Commission represents one of the best-known and most-ignored passages in Scripture.

I long for that to change. I long for these words to be applied to my life as a disciple of Jesus and in the lives of every disciple of Jesus. I long for these words to be at the center of everything we do in the church today.

With that in mind, we'll spend the next three days digging into three primary exhortations given to us from the Great Commission: (1) believe the authority of Christ, (2) obey the commands of Christ, and (3) depend on the presence of Christ.

Jesus Is Lord

Imagine you're driving down the highway and you see blue lights flashing in your rearview mirror. You look back and see a police car immediately behind you, signaling for you to pull over. What would you do?

How would you answer the previous question?

You would pull over, of course. Why? Because the police officer has the authority to command that you stop your vehicle—and the authority to punish you if you refuse. His authority would compel your obedience.

What are the primary sources of authority in your life?

How do you generally respond to people who have authority over you? Why?

When Jesus gathered His disciples to deliver the Great Commission, He didn't start by issuing a series of commands. He started with a claim that's both simple and shocking: "Jesus came to them and said, 'All authority in heaven and on earth has been given to me' " (v. 18).

Jesus' commission was a historically important moment because it set a precedent for the future—for everything the disciples would accomplish after His ascension to heaven. But Jesus' claim to have all authority in heaven and on earth was also an important connection with the past. Specifically, it connected Jesus with a major prophecy delivered centuries earlier by the prophet Daniel:

> **In my vision at night I looked, and there before me was one like a son of man, coming with the clouds of heaven. He approached the Ancient of Days and was led into his presence. He was given authority, glory and sovereign power; all peoples, nations and men of every language worshiped him. His dominion is an everlasting dominion that will not pass away, and his kingdom is one that will never be destroyed.**
> **Daniel 7:13-14**

Which words and phrases strike you as most interesting in these verses? Why?

In what ways does Daniel's prophecy point to Jesus?

First, notice again this clear expression of God's will for the world: that He wants to redeem men and women from every people group on the planet. We must understand this. Jesus' mission on earth was never about *one* nation; it was about *all* nations. In the same way, Jesus' authority doesn't apply to only *one* people group; He has authority over *all* people.

But Jesus' authority goes even further. If we believe His words, He has authority over all things— over everything we can imagine.

Read the following passages of Scripture and record what they teach about Jesus' authority.

Matthew 8:23-27

Matthew 9:1-8

Matthew 28:1-10

Do we believe this? Do we believe Jesus possesses the authority He claimed to possess? If so, we must change our lives. To be a disciple of Jesus means to live under His authority— to surrender every facet of our lives to Him. And if we surrender to His authority, we must pay attention to what He said next: "Therefore go" (28:19).

Jesus' Authority Compels Us to Go

When we think about it, engaging in evangelism, missions, and discipleship makes sense only if Jesus has authority over heaven and earth.

There are literally billions of people across this world who don't believe the gospel. Some of these people live in our communities; many of them live in Africa and northern India and China and every other country around the world. Some of these people have been exposed to the gospel message and rejected it; many others have never even heard the good news of salvation.

Despite their differences, these billions of people all have something vital in common: Jesus is their rightful Lord. Jesus is the only One who can save them from their sins. Therefore, we must go and make the gospel known.

There are two reasons we must go. First, because God loves every human being and wants every human being to experience salvation. We read in 1 Timothy 2:4 that God "wants all men to be saved and to come to a knowledge of the truth." We understand from 2 Peter 3:9 that God "is patient with [us], not wanting anyone to perish, but everyone to come to repentance."

What do you find most helpful about the previous passages of Scripture? Why?

How does knowing what God desires affect your actions and decisions?

Second, we must go and make the gospel known because Jesus alone is worthy of honor and glory and praise. We proclaim the gospel and make disciples because billions of people in this world are robbing Jesus of the glory due to Him as Lord. Billions of people are worshiping false gods and idols when they should be worshiping Jesus alone.

Because Jesus is worthy, we work to spread His name. Because Jesus is Lord, we look forward to the day when men and women "from every nation, tribe, people and language" will stand "before the throne and in front of the Lamb" (Rev. 7:9).

What's your reaction to the thought of Jesus being denied the honor He deserves?

What steps have you recently taken to glorify Jesus above all other things?

Jesus has authority over all things. That's a foundation on which we can build our lives.

THAT'S A FACT THAT SHOULD GIVE US CONFIDENCE

AS WE GO AND WORK TO ACCOMPLISH HIS WILL.

OBEY THE COMMANDS OF CHRIST

When I think of the Great Commission, I often remember a small group of Christians I had the pleasure of spending time with in a predominantly Muslim country. These brothers and sisters run a successful business that employs Muslim men and women, and they use that platform to purposefully love people and lead them to eternal life in Christ.

My friends start by sharing the gospel, which must be done wisely in a country where evangelism can lead to persecution or death. Specifically, their goal is to sew threads of the gospel into the fabric of every interaction with Muslims. In every conversation, in every business dealing, at every meal, and in every meeting, they look for opportunities to speak about who God is, how God loves, what God is doing in the world, and supremely what God has done for us in Christ.

Of course, not every conversation involves a full-on, hour-long gospel explanation. They simply try to saturate all of their interactions with various strands of the gospel—like weaving various colored threads into a quilt. Their prayer is that in time God will open the eyes of the men and women around them to behold the tapestry of the gospel and that those men and women will come to Christ.

Here's the great news: it's working. Because my friends demonstrate genuine affection and care for the people they work with and live with, they've earned the right to be heard. Because my friends offer to pray with those who are sick and take steps to help those in need, Muslims are experiencing the love of Christ. And because my friends are willing to proclaim the gospel, the people who hear them are experiencing salvation.

Who among your friends and family does a good job of weaving the gospel message into everyday life?

When have you recently been successful at doing so? What happened next?

As I think about my friends—simple followers of Christ living alongside one another and working to make disciples and multiply churches—I can't help but wonder, *Why don't we all do this?* Obviously, the situation and circumstances are different in each of our lives, but isn't that a good thing? What if God has placed every one of us in different locations with different jobs and different gifts around different people for the distinct purpose that every single one of us would make disciples and multiply churches?

What's your reaction to the previous questions? Why?

That's the way God has called us to live. Yesterday we focused on Jesus' first statement in the Great Commission: "All authority in heaven and on earth has been given to me" (Matt. 28:18). Because of that authority, Jesus' second statement demands obedience:

> **Therefore go and make disciples of all nations, baptizing them in the name of the Father and of the Son and of the Holy Spirit, and teaching them to obey everything I have commanded you. Matthew 28:19-20**

This isn't a suggestion. It's a command for every disciple of Christ, including you and me, to make disciples of Christ.

Share the Word

One question you may be pondering right now is *how?* How do we actually go about making disciples? There are several steps we can take based on Matthew 28:19, and the first is to go. We're not simply called to sit comfortably in the same seat Sunday after Sunday and listen to sermons. Rather, we're called to actively live as followers of Jesus in our families, communities, workplaces, and so on.

As we go, we're called to share the Word of God. We're called to speak about the gospel even as we live according to the gospel. We're called to proclaim with our words and our actions that Jesus is Lord.

Now this doesn't mean we need to walk up to a coworker at the water cooler and say, "You're a damned and dreadful sinner in need of salvation." A better approach is to follow the example of my friends as I described them earlier: to sew the threads of the gospel into our lives whenever we get the opportunity.

When have you offended someone by sharing the gospel or speaking the truth from God's Word? What happened next?

Practically, this means we talk about God as someone we know, love, and worship. Instead of speaking like atheists, attributing circumstances around us to chance or coincidence, let's put God's character on display every day before people who may not yet believe in Him. Let's speak about God as Creator, as Judge, and as Savior in the context of our everyday conversations.

To what degree do you currently weave theological truths into your everyday conversations? Explain.

What obstacles prevent you from inserting more gospel threads into your daily interactions with people?

As Christians, we should also talk about the difficulties in this world with a spirit of deep hope and unusual joy. Every trial we face, no matter how difficult, is an occasion to point people to God-given satisfaction that supersedes suffering in this life.

Most importantly, let's speak clearly and compassionately about the Person and work of Jesus. Let's talk about His life—the people He healed, the things He taught, the miracles He performed, and the ways He served. Let's speak about His death. Let's proclaim His resurrection.

What do the people around you know about your relationship with Jesus?

What can your friends and acquaintances learn about you, based on the way you react to suffering? Explain.

Teach the Word

According to the Great Commission, followers of Jesus are called to go, make disciples, and teach those disciples to obey everything Jesus commanded. Notice that disciple making involves more than just leading people to trust in Christ; disciple making also involves teaching people to follow Christ.

Also notice that Matthew 28:19 mentions baptism as an essential element of this teaching. We baptize new disciples because doing so symbolizes their identification with the Person of Christ and their inclusion in the body of Christ. It helps them understand what they've experienced even as they publicly announce their intention to follow Jesus.

What opportunities do you have to experience the baptism of new believers?

What emotions do you experience when you witness people being baptized? Why?

In today's society most people associate teaching with the idea of transferring information from one person (a teacher) to many people (students). That's what happens in school, after all.

But this isn't how teaching should be understood in the body of Christ—not exclusively, anyway. There's a place for books and classes and intellectual knowledge, but it's much more valuable for an experienced disciple of Christ to show others what the life of Christ looks like in action.

What are the dangers of relying only on intellectual knowledge when teaching others how to follow Christ?

How can you avoid these dangers?

Some might say, "Isn't that what preachers are supposed to do—teach the Word of God?" In one sense the answer is yes. God has clearly called and gifted some people in the church to teach His Word *formally*. At the same time, He's commanded all of us in the church to teach His Word *relationally*.

In the Great Commission Jesus told all of His disciples to go, baptize, and teach people to obey everything He'd commanded them. This kind of teaching doesn't require a special gift or a specific setting. It happens all over the place—in homes, in neighborhoods, in workplaces, on car rides, in meetings, and over meals—in the context of where we live, work, and play every day.

We'll explore this in more detail throughout this week's Personal Disciple-Making Plan.

Read the following passages of Scripture and record what they say about methods for teaching others how to follow Christ.

Deuteronomy 6:4-9

1 Corinthians 10:31–11:1

1 Thessalonians 1:4-7

Identify one way you can teach the Word to someone in the pattern of your everyday life.

If you want to live as a disciple of Jesus, you must give your life to the work of making disciples. You must be willing to share the Word of God with those who need to hear it.

AND YOU MUST BE WILLING TO TEACH THE WAYS

OF GOD TO THOSE WHO WISH TO FOLLOW HIM.

DEPEND ON THE PRESENCE OF CHRIST

Do you remember how Matthew introduced Jesus at the beginning of his Gospel? He started by writing a long genealogy showing that Jesus is "the son of David, the son of Abraham" (1:1).

This was important because it emphasized how Jesus fulfilled God's promise to Abraham that "all peoples on earth will be blessed through you" (Gen. 12:3). In the same way, Jesus was of the royal line of David. He fulfilled God's promise to David that "your house and your kingdom will endure forever before me; your throne will be established forever" (2 Sam. 7:16).

So Matthew made it clear from the beginning of his Gospel that Jesus is a big deal. Jesus is royalty. Jesus is the inheritor of ancient promises and a blessing for the world. Jesus is Lord, a title that corresponds to His proclamation at the end of Matthew's Gospel that "all authority in heaven and on earth has been given to me" (28:18).

And yet even in the midst of this glorious introduction, Matthew also paved the way for us to understand that Jesus isn't aloof and distant from us. Rather, He's near. He's with us and for us:

> **All this took place to fulfill what the Lord had said through the prophet: "The virgin will be with child and will give birth to a son, and they will call him Immanuel"—which means, "God with us." Matthew 1:22-23**

"God with us." Keep that idea in mind, because it sets up a powerful connection with the conclusion of Jesus' Great Commission at the end of Matthew's Gospel:

> **Go and make disciples of all nations, baptizing them in the name of the Father and of the Son and of the Holy Spirit, and teaching them to obey everything I have commanded you. *And surely I am with you always, to the very end of the age.* Matthew 28:19-20, emphasis added**

How does knowing that Jesus is "with us" and "with you always" impact your approach to everyday life? How should it impact your approach to everyday life?

As disciples of Jesus, we believe in the authority of Christ. And because we believe, we seek to obey the commands of Christ. In order to do that, however, we must depend on the presence of Christ as we follow Him.

Christ's Presence Fuels Our Mission

Jesus has promised to be with us always, even to the end of the age. Don't miss the importance of that promise. Because for those of us who choose to follow Christ, our mission isn't based on who we are or what we can do. It's not based on what we bring to the table.

Rather, our mission is based on who Jesus is and what He's able to do in and through our lives.

What's your reaction to the previous statement? Why?

In recent decades many people have made a big deal about spiritual gifts in the church—and rightfully so. The Bible is clear that, as Christians, we've all been equipped with specific aptitudes and abilities that help us serve the body of Christ and contribute to God's kingdom.

Read 1 Corinthians 12:7-10. Summarize what you've been taught about spiritual gifts and how they contribute to God's kingdom.

What are your primary spiritual gifts?

How have you been able to use your gifts in recent months to serve God's kingdom?

When I say that our mission as followers of Christ isn't based on what we bring to the table, it's not my intention to minimize the value of spiritual gifts. Rather, I want us to recognize that Jesus and His Spirit are the source of those gifts. As Paul made clear, it's only through His presence that our gifts have any value:

There are different kinds of gifts, but the same Spirit. There are different kinds of service, but the same Lord. There are different kinds of working, but the same God works all of them in all men. 1 Corinthians 12:4-6

No matter how gifted we may be or how dedicated we are to the church and the mission of making disciples, we can accomplish nothing without the presence of Christ working in us. That's why it's such an amazing gift that Jesus has promised to remain within us through the presence of the Holy Spirit:

I will ask the Father, and he will give you another Counselor to be with you forever—the Spirit of truth. The world cannot accept him, because it neither sees him nor knows him. But you know him, for he lives with you and will be in you. I will not leave you as orphans; I will come to you. John 14:16-18

To what degree do you rely on God's Spirit as you seek to follow Christ? Explain.

What obstacles prevent you from relying more heavily on the Holy Spirit? How can those obstacles be removed?

When we walk in the presence of Christ, we experience "him who is able to do immeasurably more than all we ask or imagine, according to his power that is at work within us" (Eph. 3:20). We experience this reality in our lives as individuals and in our churches.

So let's put down our small dreams. Let's put down our worldly ambitions and our misguided attempts to do things our own way. Let's give Christ a blank check with our lives and see where He leads through His presence in us.

Prayer and Salvation

As we walk in the presence of Christ, we'll have opportunities to make new disciples of Jesus. We'll have the privilege of inviting people to turn from their sin and trust in Jesus as Savior and Lord. This won't happen because of our cleverness or evangelistic prowess; it will happen because of the convicting work of the Holy Spirit.

But how should we handle these moments on a practical level? What should we say and what should we do when God grants us the privilege of harvesting a new follower of Christ?

How have you been taught to lead people through a salvation experience?

Do you feel confident with the ways you help people call on the Lord for salvation? Explain.

Prayer is a right and biblical response to the gospel. When you share the gospel, it's good to invite people to call out for God to save them. At the same time, it's unnecessary (and in some ways unhelpful) to tell people what they must say in order to be saved.

If, after hearing the gospel clearly and fully, people see God for who He is, their sin for what it is, and Christ for who He is and what He's done, and if they're willing to repent and believe in Jesus—to turn from their sin and to trust in Him as Savior and Lord—then there are no particular words they need to recite. There's no added value in asking them to repeat certain words after you say them.

Rather, the Spirit of God has awakened their hearts to the gospel of God, He enables them to repent and believe—to cry out for His mercy as they submit to His majesty. So encourage them to do so at that moment. And in some cases it may actually be best to encourage people to be alone with God so that you won't unknowingly, unintentionally, or unhelpfully manipulate a decision, circumstance, or situation.

Basically, as you call others to submit to the Person of Christ, you can trust the Spirit of Christ to bring them to salvation. In the same way you've committed to depend on the presence of Christ as His disciple, allow new believers to depend on His presence as they choose to follow Him.

What's your reaction to the previous statements? Why?

Finally and perhaps most importantly, once someone repents and believes in Christ, be willing to lead that person as a new follower of Christ.

REMEMBER, OUR GOAL ISN'T TO COUNT DECISIONS;
OUR GOAL IS TO MAKE DISCIPLES—AND TO DO SO THROUGH
THE PRESENCE AND POWER OF GOD'S SPIRIT IN US.

DAY 4

PERSONAL DISCIPLE-MAKING PLAN: HOW TO MAKE DISCIPLE MAKERS AMONG A FEW PEOPLE

I've mentioned several times throughout this study that God wills for disciples of Christ to make disciples from among all nations; that's our mission in this world. But I also realize that mission represents a daunting task. How can we realistically spread the gospel to every people group on the planet?

When we think about it, however, the answer to that question is surprisingly simple. Of all the men and women who've ever lived on the earth, Jesus was the most passionate about spreading God's glory to all peoples. And what did He do? He spent His life investing in a few people. His strategy for reaching all peoples was clear: make disciple makers among a few people.

As we've seen, God leads us to live in all kinds of different places throughout the world. Yet regardless of where we live and what we do for a living, our task is the same. Whether you're a pastor who leads a church or a mother who works at home, whether you're in the mountains of northern Afghanistan or the plains of midwestern America, God has commanded every disciple to make disciples. No Christian is excused from this command, and no Christian would want to escape this command.

So every one of us must look around and ask, *How will I make disciple makers among a few people?* This is a vital question, and I've broken it down into four smaller questions in order to help you move forward in making disciples who make disciples.

How Will You Bring Them In?

Making disciple makers starts with identifying a small group of men or women who are willing to make disciples of their own. (I say "men or women" because it's been my experience that disciple making is best done with men together and women together rather than mixing genders.) So consider two, three, or four people God has put in your sphere of influence whom you can lead to make disciples.

Make a list of people in your sphere of influence who try to live as disciples of Christ.

Which of these individuals would be interested in meeting with you for the purpose of growing as followers of Christ?

Don't be afraid to seek God's help in this process. Ask Him for the names of specific people you could lead to make disciples. If you're having trouble identifying people, ask a pastor or leader in your church for help.

When you've identified that small group of people, invite them to spend intentional time with you in the days ahead for the express purpose of growing in Christ together.

Write down the names of the people to whom you will send this invitation.

How Will You Teach Them to Obey?

Part of disciple making includes teaching people to obey everything Christ has commanded. So think through how this will happen with the few people you identified earlier.

What do you need to teach your group from God's Word? What essential doctrines and Scripture passages will you discuss?

How can you teach your group in a way that helps them learn to read and understand God's Word for themselves?

Regardless of what methods you choose, don't settle for simply teaching information. Instead, focus on seeing these disciples' transformation. When you gather together, ask questions about how they're following Christ and fishing for men. You might start by using the six primary topics from this study's Personal Disciple-Making Plan to help your group develop their own plans for being and making disciples. These topics could then become a basis for you to ask them (and for them to ask you) how they're following Jesus and whom they're telling about Jesus.

As we've seen, this kind of grace-saturated, gospel-driven mutual accountability is absolutely essential to being disciples and making disciples.

How will you communicate the need for accountability to the people you lead?

How will you incorporate mutual accountability into your time together?

How Will You Model Obedience?

This is where disciple making gets both interesting and invigorating. We've seen in Matthew 4 that Jesus has called us to follow Him. Yet once we do this and we begin fishing for men, we find ourselves in a position where we're now leading other people to follow us.

Paul said to the Corinthian Christians, "Follow my example, as I follow the example of Christ" (1 Cor. 11:1). He told the Philippian Christians, "Whatever you have learned or received or heard from me, or seen in me—put it into practice. And the God of peace will be with you" (Phil. 4:9). Paul had so faithfully lived a life of obedient discipleship in front of these believers that he could say, "Follow my example."

Do you feel you're an example worth imitating when it comes to living as a follower of Christ? Explain.

These verses don't imply that Paul was perfect, and we definitely don't have to be perfect to make disciples. But as you focus your life on the few people God has given you, they need to see and hear and sense the life of Christ in you. So invite them into your home. Let them see you with your family. Show them how to pray, study the Bible, and share the gospel.

What obstacles prevent you from more fully sharing your life with other believers?

What steps can you take to intentionally invite those you're discipling to live the Christian life and minister with you?

Do you see how God has arranged this? In order to show others how to effectively study the Bible, we must be studying the Bible. In order to help others proclaim the gospel, we must be proclaiming the gospel. That's why this process of making disciple makers is so transformative for everyone involved.

Practically, making disciple makers involves looking at these few people and saying to them, "Follow me." So plan intentional ways to model what it means to follow Christ.

How Will You Send Them Out?

As you teach the commands of Christ and model the life of Christ, one of the commands you're teaching and modeling is Jesus' command to make disciples. The goal isn't just for these few people you're focused on to follow Jesus; the goal is for them to fish for men.

So the time will come when you'll need to commission those few to find a few people of their own. By then you'll have shown them what it means to make disciples, and you'll send them out to do the same.

How will you work with God's Spirit to evaluate when people are ready to be sent out to make more disciple makers?

What steps can you take to prepare people for their eventual commission?

Of course, you'll continue to encourage, serve, teach, care for, and pray for those you've discipled, but you'll also release them to make disciples as you've done. In this way, your life will literally begin to multiply the gospel in the world through the disciples you've made.

Your circumstances and my circumstances are vastly different, yet our goal is the same:

DECIDE TO SPEND YOUR LIFE MAKING

DISCIPLE MAKERS AMONG A FEW PEOPLE.

PERSONAL DISCIPLE-MAKING PLAN: HOW TO SPREAD GOD'S GLORY AMONG ALL PEOPLES

The eternal purpose of God is to save people through Christ. The clear commission of Christ for every disciple is to make disciples, not just generally but of all nations—disciples from every people group in the world.

Yesterday you developed plans for making disciple makers among a few people, but that doesn't mean you should turn a blind eye toward the rest of the world. No, regardless of where you live, you must ask how your life will impact every nation, tribe, tongue, and people in the world. This isn't a question for extraordinary missionaries; this is a question for ordinary disciples.

What's your reaction to the previous statements? Why?

So consider the following ways you can play a part in spreading God's glory to the ends of the earth.

How Will You Pray for the Nations?

From our knees in our homes, you and I have an opportunity to be a part of what God is doing around the world. So let's pray passionately for God's kingdom to come and His will to be done throughout the earth.

How will you pray for the nations during your regular encounters with God and His Word?

How can you use current events and news sources to spur your prayers for all peoples?

Many people have had success using a tool like Operation World (*www.operationworld.org*) as a way to pray for every nation in the world. Regardless of your method, plan to deliberately focus your prayers on the nations generally, as well as on specific unreached people groups around the world.

What steps will you take to begin praying for specific people groups who've not yet received the good news about Jesus?

How Will You Give to the Nations?

Researchers estimate that Christians in North America give an average of 2.5 percent of their income to a local church (which I think is probably a generous estimate, but we'll go with it).[1] These local churches then give an average of about 2 percent of those funds to spread the gospel overseas. In other words, for every $100 that a professing Christian earns in North America, he or she gives $.05 through the local church to the rest of the world. Simply put, this can't be the case among authentic followers of Jesus.

On average, what percentage of your income do you give away for the good of God's kingdom?

What percentage of your church's resources is given to spread the gospel overseas?

God has given His people worldly wealth for one purpose: to spread His worship worldwide. Disciples of Jesus live simply and give sacrificially because we want the glory of Christ in all nations more than we want nicer comforts, newer possessions, and greater luxuries.

What's your reaction to the previous statements? Why?

As a Christian, how will you sacrifice the wants in your budget in order to give to the needs of the world—most particularly, the need for every people group to hear the gospel? As a member of a church, how will you lead your church to cut programs and priorities that you once thought were important to help meet the physical needs of starving brothers and sisters and the spiritual needs of unreached men and women all over the world?

What are you willing to sacrifice in order to give more of your resources to help spread the gospel among all peoples?

How can you work to ensure that your church is investing wisely to meet the needs of unreached people all over the world?

As a follower of Christ, plan to sacrifice and spend for the sake of the nations.

How Will You Go to the Nations?

Strategically, creatively, and wisely consider ways you can share the gospel with other people groups—particularly those that are unreached (meaning they have no access to the gospel). Some of these people groups have come to America and may be in your community, so consider ways you can reach out to them, whether they're Somali Muslims, Egyptian Arabs, Tibetan Buddhists, or any other people group around you.

Where are the pockets of unreached peoples in your community?

How can you gain a greater understanding of these people groups—their needs, their cultures, their stories, and so on?

Next, consider ways you can cross the ocean and go to people who need to hear the gospel. This may be a short-term trip for a week or two, a midterm endeavor for a year or two, or a long-term commitment for a decade or two. Consider all of the avenues through which you might spend your life, lead your family, or leverage your work in order to penetrate the people groups of the world with the gospel—because this is what you were created to do.

What opportunities does your church provide to help people go to the nations?

How will you work with God's Spirit to determine your future involvement in spreading the gospel to all nations?

The King's Call

We're followers of Jesus. We've died to ourselves, and we now live in Christ. He has saved us from our sins and has satisfied our souls. He has transformed our minds with His truth, fulfilled our desires with His joy, and conformed our ways to His will.

He has joined us together in bodies of believers called local churches to accomplish one all-consuming commission: the declaration of His gospel and the display of His glory to all peoples of the world.

This task involves all of us. God doesn't intend any of His children to be sidelined as spectators in the Great Commission. He's called each one to be on the front lines of the supreme mission in all of history. Every disciple of Jesus has been called, loved, created, and saved to make disciples of Jesus, who make disciples of Jesus, who make disciples of Jesus—until the grace of God is enjoyed and the glory of God is exalted among every people group on the planet.

On that day every disciple of Jesus—every follower of Christ and fisher of men—will see the Savior's face and behold the Father's splendor in a scene of indescribable beauty and everlasting bliss that will never fade away.

THIS IS A CALL WORTH DYING FOR.

THIS IS A KING WORTH LIVING FOR.

1. John Ronsvalle and Sylvia Ronsvalle, *The State of Church Giving Through 2004: Will We Will?* 16th ed. (Champaign, IL: Empty Tomb, 2006), 36.

DEVOTED TO
CHRIST.
SERVING THE
CHURCH.
REACHING THE
NATIONS.

+R

Radical.net

a resource ministry of
pastor and author
David Platt

SECRET CHURCH

KNOW HIS WORD. KNOW HIS PERSECUTED.

Shhh. Tell everyone.

WHAT'S SO RADICAL ABOUT FOLLOWING JESUS?

When Jesus called His disciples, they left everything and followed Him. He expects no less of His followers today.

In this six-session Bible study, David Platt challenges the notion that Christians can follow Jesus without giving up our old way of life. Redeemed by radical grace, we're called to a radical abandonment of our agendas, to a radical strategy for making disciples, and to a radical vision for being on mission.

Jesus is calling you out of comfortable Christianity to take up your cross and follow Him. To embrace Him as your richest treasure. To feed the poor and reach the lost. To live for the glory of God.

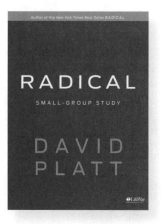

THAT'S RADICAL.

Member Book, item 005471378
Leader Kit, item 005471377

WWW.LIFEWAY.COM